COLLINS GEM

G000108063

Rowenna Stuart

HarperCollins*Publishers*

HarperCollins Publishers
PO Box, Glasgow G4 0NB

Created and produced by
The Printer's Devil, Glasgow

First published 1998

Reprint 10 9 8 7 6 5 4 3 2 1

© The Printer's Devil, 1998

ISBN 0 00 472156 X

Printed in Italy by Amadeus S.p.A.

CONTENTS

Introduction	9
The History of the Tarot	13
The Structure of the Tarot	20
The Minor Arcana	22
The Major Arcana	31
Card Numerology	34
The Dignity of the Cards	36
Using the Cards	38
Choosing Your Deck	38
Keeping and Handling Your Cards	39
Preparing for a Reading	42
Choosing Which Spread to Use	43
Shuffling and Selecting the Cards	44
Laying Out the Cards	47
Interpreting the Spread	49
Some Words of Advice	58
Spreads	60
3-Card Spread	60

7-Card Horseshoe Spread   62
6-Card Spread   64
Yes/No Spread   66
Question and Answer Spread   68
7-Card Infinity Spread   70
21-Card Spread   72
Choices Spread   74
Alchemist's Spread   76
Celtic Cross Spread   78

The Meaning of the Cards   81
  The Major Arcana
    The Fool   82
    The Magician   84
    The High Priestess   86
    The Empress   88
    The Emperor   90
    The Pope   92
    The Lovers   94
    The Chariot   96
    Justice   98
    The Hermit   100
    The Wheel of Fortune   102

Strength   104
The Hanged Man   106
Death   108
Temperance   110
The Devil   112
The Tower   114
The Star   116
The Moon   118
The Sun   120
Judgement   122
The World   124
The Minor Arcana
    The Suit of Wands   126
    The Suit of Cups   156
    The Suit of Swords   186
    The Suit of Coins   216

Further Reading   247

Useful Addresses   251

For
Michael,
Olivia and Victoria

ACKNOWLEDGEMENTS

I would like to thank the many people who, in their own different ways, have all helped bring this book into being.

My greatest thanks are due to Carol Shaw and her team at The Printer's Devil for providing me with the opportunity to write it in the first place and for producing it so efficiently and attractively. I am also indebted to my friend, mentor and fellow reader, Eleanor Hunter, for her advice and helpful suggestions not only on this but on many tarot-related matters over the years.

I extend my gratitude to Stephen Tolley of Carta Mundi (UK) for the supply of the cards, and to Bobbie Bensaid of U.S. Games and Geoffrey (Tailor) for their perseverance in the face of my requests for permissions, illustrative matter and props.

Lastly (but certainly not least), for their patience and toleration of the endless disruption and inconvenience during my writing, my family deserve more thanks than I can ever record.

INTRODUCTION

It's only human nature to want to know what the future holds for us – romance? wealth? happiness? – and every year thousands of people turn to fortune-tellers to provide them with some glimpse of Things to Come.

Tarot reading, in particular, has become very popular in recent years, perhaps because of the air of mystery and the exotic that surrounds the cards themselves. It was precisely this which in a more superstitious age saw tarot cards condemned and outlawed as 'the Devil's Picture Book' and even today, they are still regarded with suspicion in certain quarters.

Such fears are born of ignorance, for anyone who learns anything about tarot quickly realises that there is nothing intrinsically sinister or potentially malevolent in the cards. Rather, tarot cards work, not by invoking occult entities or indulging in magic but by providing

THE HISTORY OF THE TAROT

No one knows for certain when, and from where, tarot cards originated. Ancient Egypt is often cited as their source, as is China, but in fact India is a much more likely origin for what became the tarot, which was then brought to medieval Europe by the gypsies. Gypsies began migrating from their Asian homelands in the 9th century and reached central Europe some five or six hundred years later. They brought with them their Hindu religious beliefs and customs, one of which involved the keeping of religious texts on cards bound together by string. These sacred books of cards were highly decorated with illustrations and symbols designed to explain the basic elements of the faith to an illiterate audience. It is from these that the tarot deck, much as we know it today, emerged in the 14th century. As the gypsies continued to migrate throughout Europe, so too did the tarot, used both as a fortune-telling device and also for playing card games.

In Venice and Piedmont in northern Italy around this time, a particularly popular card game was *tarocco* or *tarrochi*. It was usually played by three people and involved bidding, point-scoring

A 16th-century woodcarving depicting a tarot reading

and trick-taking, not unlike today's bridge. The
deck used had 78 cards: four suits (known as the
Minor Arcana), each comprising 10 numbered

cards plus 4 court cards, together with a further 22 illustrated cards. These picture cards, which were known as trumps, triumphs or collectively as the Major Arcana, were decorated with fascinating and mysterious imagery: men hanging upside down by their feet, women wrestling with lions, female popes, people falling from lightning-struck towers. At a time when the Church sought to root out and exterminate any hint of unorthodox beliefs with its Holy Inquisition, it is easy to see why tarot decks were consistently condemned and outlawed as 'the Devil's picturebook'. In spite

The strange imagery of the tarot

of this, tarot decks continued to be produced, with several different styles evolving: the Florentine tarot, for example, contained 97 cards while the Bolognese tarot contained only 62.

By the late 18th century, tarot divination was particularly popular in France, perhaps because of the uncertainty of the revolutionary times. Indeed, one of the most popular and influential of all decks, the Tarot de Marseilles was originally published in France about this time although its imagery is much older, as can be seen from the selection of Major Arcana cards from this deck shown opposite; this deck is also used in this book to illustrate the sections describing the specific meanings of the cards. It was during this period that the names of the Major Arcana cards adopted their now traditional French titles. This was due in no small part to the influence of French occultists such as Antoine Court de Gébelin (1723–87) and Etteilla who, in their writings and in the tarot decks they created, first suggested tarot's links with Ancient Egyptian mysticism and made a connection between the Major Arcana cards and the Jewish mystical tradition of the Qaballah (see also p.35). These views were taken up, refined and expanded during the course of the 19th century by esoterics such as Eliphas Lévi (1810–1875), Gerard

The quasi-medieval imagery of the Tarot de Marseilles

Encausse 'Papus' (1865–1917) and Oswald Wirth (1860– 1943), all of whose work has contributed greatly to tarot tradition.

However, perhaps the most enduring influence on the way cards are used and interpreted has been the work of the Hermetic Order of the Golden Dawn, a secret occult society which operated in London between 1888 and 1900. The O.G.D. – whose members included such leading literary figures of the day as W. B. Yeats, Bram Stoker,

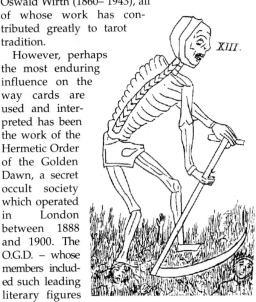

The trump card, Death, as depicted in the 1781 edition of Court de Gébelin's Le Monde Primitif.

A.E., Algernon Blackwood and Sax Rohmer –
believed that the tarot was the key to a unified
esoteric system that linked astrology, ritual magic,
numerology and the Qaballah. Two of the Order's
members, Arthur Waite and Pamela Colman
Smith, later produced the revolutionary Rider-
Waite deck. This deck has gone on to become one
of the most popular decks in the world and many
subsequently designed decks are clearly derived
from it, especially in the design of their Minor
Arcana cards. Another O.G.D. member, Aleister
Crowley (1875–1947), also produced a highly
influential deck, the Thoth Tarot.

In recent years there has been a dramatic
upsurge in popular interest in the tarot. New tarot
decks are being created at an unprecedented rate,
some based on traditional Western influences
while others attempt to draw on a broader range
of cultures, wisdoms, and histories. As the new
millennium dawns, there is little doubt that tarot
will continue to attract new adherents, for whom
the following chapters will – I hope – prove to be
an engaging and stimulating introduction.

THE STRUCTURE OF THE TAROT

As we saw in the previous chapter, as the Tarot developed during the Middle Ages, packs comprising differing numbers of cards evolved. Today's standard deck has fixed upon the 78-card variant that was common in northern Italy in the 16th century.

The 78 cards are divided into two distinct sections or arcana (which means 'mysteries' or 'secrets'):

✴ the 22 cards of the Major Arcana

✴ the 56 cards of the Minor Arcana

It could be argued that each of these sets actually comprises a separate deck, and some readers do use spreads that involve the Major Arcana cards alone, although it is more common to perform readings using the entire deck. However, as the terms 'major' and 'minor' suggest, the two arcana are not equal; the difference between them lies in the diffferent aspects of human existence that each depicts.

The cards of the Major Arcana represent the major issues in the life of the Querant (literally, the questioner – the person for whom the reading is being done). They depict those fundamental principles and experiences that are at the core of human life: spirituality, theories about life and death, ethical dilemmas and judgements, personal morality, interactions both with our fellow humans and with our environment. Some commentators actually represent the Major Arcana as something akin to a spiritual map, the means by which the Querant will be able to judge the progress of their inner self on the journey through life to death and beyond. Others interpret these cards as representations of elemental forces underlying the Querant's life, forces over which he or she has no control and which are loosely described as the actions of destiny or fate.

In contrast, the cards of the Minor Arcana are seen as depicting the more mundane and superficial occurrences in the Querant's life, together with his or her reactions to them: the incidents, events, experiences and people that are part of a person's everyday existence. When doing a reading however, the distinctions between the two arcana tend to be less evident as the different cards interact with each other to create a seamless symbolic picture of the

Querant's life and the various influences in it.

THE MINOR ARCANA

The 56 cards of the Minor Arcana are the direct ancestors of our contemporary playing cards and, like them, are further divided into four suits:

✴ Wands (or Rods or Batons)

✴ Cups

✴ Swords

✴ Coins (or Pentacles or Discs)

Note that the name of some of the suits can vary depending on the particular deck.

Each of these suits corresponds to a suit of a conventional playing card pack:

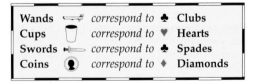

Wands	⟶ *correspond to*	♣ **Clubs**
Cups	*correspond to*	♥ **Hearts**
Swords	⟶ *correspond to*	♣ **Spades**
Coins	*correspond to*	♦ **Diamonds**

The Suits

Each tarot suit comprises:

* 10 'pip' cards (numbered from Ace to Ten)

* 4 court cards (Page, Knight, Queen and King)

Each of the non-court cards originally only contained patterns of the appropriate number of suit symbols or 'pips' (eight cups, six swords, etc., similar to contemporary playing cards). However, this tradition was broken in 1910 by Pamela Colman Smith, the illustrator of the famous Rider-Waite deck. In this ground-breaking deck, she drew each of the pip cards with a scene that was designed to act as an *aide-mémoire* for the reader and so simplify the interpretation of the cards. The Rider-Waite deck has gone on to become one of the most popular decks in the world and many subsequently designed decks are clearly derived from it, especially in the design of their Minor Arcana cards.

Just as the suit names vary from deck to deck, so do the names given to the court cards. In some modern decks, the Page is often replaced by the Princess in order to balance out the gender bias of the traditional depiction. In other decks, particularly those based on non-Western cultures, the names of the court cards are totally changed and if you are using one of these decks it is important to establish which card is which before consulting the interpretations given for these cards later in the book.

Attributions

Each of the cards in a tarot deck has a series of specific characteristics and associations known as attributions. These attributions are the essential building blocks of the tarot as they impart to each card the unique qualities which are the basis of all interpretations of them. Much of the symbolism of the tarot is also bound up with, and explained by, these attributions.

For the Minor Arcana, attributions are assigned primarily to each of the suits. Thus, each suit represents a combination of:

✳ a particular area of everday experience

✳ three of the signs of the Zodiac

✳ one of the four Aristotelian elements of Fire, Water, Air or Earth (which were once believed to be the sole components of all substances in the universe)

✳ a gender principle (that is, it is either masculine or feminine).

The attributions for each of the suits is given in the following table.

Suit	Life Experience	Zodiac Signs	Element	Gender
	Career	Leo Aries Sagittarius	Fire	Masc.
	Emotions	Pisces Cancer Scorpio	Water	Fem.
	Intellectual activity	Gemini Libra Aquarius	Air	Masc.
	Material aspects	Taurus Capricorn Virgo	Earth	Fem.

Gender Principles

While the first three attribution categories are easily understood, it is perhaps worth expanding upon the principles underlying the gender attribution since the meanings of 'masculine' and 'feminine' in the context of the tarot differ from the more conventional interpretations of the terms.

The belief that there are two equal and opposing forces or principles constantly at work in the universe has been a fundamental component of a wide variety of philosophies and belief systems stretching back over very many centuries and across many different cultures. The 'masculine' principle is traditionally seen as positive, rational, assertive, creative and active, while the feminine principle is negative, introverted, destructive and passive.

Although framed in sexual terms, it is

homme

femme

important to realise that these principles are not describing the personality traits stereotypically associated with men and women. Rather, they are the collective terms for a series of opposing qualities common to everyone (regardless of gender) and every situation. There is also no suggestion that one principle is superior or better than the other: they are complementary and if present in equal force, produce balance and harmony in individuals or their lives. However, much of the philosophy and symbolism of the tarot is concerned with the potential imbalance between these forces, the tension this causes and how it is resolved (or not).

The Court Arcana

The court cards (referred to collectively as the court arcana) generally represent people – either the Querant or individuals with whom he or she interacts. Identifying precisely who these people might be in a spread can be quite tricky but some clues can be found as the court arcana take the attributions associated with their particular suit. Thus, for example, a Wand court card might suggest a creative extrovert born under the signs of Leo, Aries or Sagittarius. Additional, more specific attributions for these cards can be applied when choosing a Significator (see below). However, the situation can be further confused by the realisation that at times the court cards (particularly the Knights and Pages) will represent situations rather than individuals with no obvious pointer as to which may be being referred to in a spread. In short, the interpretation of the court arcana is fraught with difficulties and it may be necessary to consider a number of possible explanations of them, taking into account other cards in the spread.

Significators

A common – though by no means universal – practice prior to doing a reading is to select a Significator, a card that will specifically represent the Querant during the reading. The court cards alone are used for this purpose and the actual choice of card is traditionally governed by a number of factors, principally:

* the astrological sign of the Querant

* his or her age

* his or her physical appearance

The full range of Significator categories are outlined in the following tables.

WANDS

Card	Zodiac Sign	Age	Appearance
King	Aries, Leo, Sagittarius	Male over 35 years	Red/Blonde hair Hazel/Grey eyes
Queen	Aries, Leo, Sagittarius	Female over 35 years	Red/Blonde hair Brown/Blue eyes
Knight	Aries, Leo, Sagittarius	Male under 35 years	Blonde hair Grey/Blue eyes
Page	Aries, Leo, Sagittarius	Young boy or girl	Red/Blonde hair Blue eyes

CUPS

Card	Zodiac Sign	Age	Appearance
King	Pisces, Cancer, Scorpio	Male over 35 years	Fair hair Blue eyes
Queen	Pisces, Cancer, Scorpio	Female over 35 years	Golden brown hair Blue eyes
Knight	Pisces, Cancer, Scorpio	Male under 35 years	Brown hair Grey/Blue eyes
Page	Pisces, Cancer, Scorpio	Young boy or girl	Brown hair Blue/Brown eyes

SWORDS

Card	Zodiac Sign	Age	Appearance
King	Gemini, Libra, Aquarius	Male over 35 years	Black hair Dark eyes
Queen	Gemini, Libra, Aquarius	Female over 35 years	Light Brown hair Grey eyes
Knight	Gemini, Libra, Aquarius	Male under 35 years	Dark Brown hair Dark eyes
Page	Gemini, Libra, Aquarius	Young boy or girl	Light Brown hair Blue eyes

COINS

Card	Zodiac Sign	Age	Appearance
King	Taurus, Virgo, Capricorn	Male over 35 years	Black/Dk Brown hair Dark eyes
Queen	Taurus, Virgo, Capricorn	Female over 35 years	Black/Dk Brown hair Dark eyes
Knight	Taurus, Virgo, Capricorn	Male under 35 years	Brown hair Dark eyes
Page	Taurus, Virgo, Capricorn	Young boy or girl	Brown hair Dark eyes

It can of course be difficult to match a Querant precisely with all the attributes of a particular court card and readers usually compromise by choosing a combination of some of the categories that seem to fit the Querant best. For example, the Knight of Coins might be selected as the Significator of a young, dark-haired man or the Queen of Wands for a mature Sagittarian woman. Like so much concerning tarot, there are no hard-and-fast rules and each reader usually evolves a system for choosing a Significator that they feel comfortable with on the basis of their own experience.

Once chosen, the Significator can either be removed from the deck and placed face up on the table to provide a focus for the reading or else left in the deck. Once the cards are split, only that portion containing the Significator is used for the reading.

THE MAJOR ARCANA

As outlined previously, the 22 pictorial cards which comprise the Major Arcana are considered the most important cards in the deck, representing the fundamental precepts and motivations of the Querant's life. The imagery on the cards tradition-ally depicts archetypes, that is, highly symbolic figures that are universally recognised and understood across a broad spectrum of religions, mythologies and folk cultures. The sequence of the Major Arcana cards is listed below:

0	The Fool	11	Strength
1	The Magician	12	The Hanged Man
2	The High Priestess	13	Death
3	The Empress	14	Temperance
4	The Emperor	15	The Devil
5	The Pope	16	The Tower
6	The Lovers	17	The Star
7	The Chariot	18	The Moon
8	Justice	19	The Sun
9	The Hermit	20	Judgement
10	The Wheel of Fortune	21	The World

Note that a number of variations on this sequence can be encountered, depending on the particular deck you are using: in some decks, most notably the Rider-Waite and those derived from it, The Pope is titled The Hierophant, and Justice and Strength are transposed (that is, are numbered 11 and 8 respectively); in others The Fool is positioned as number 22 (although the card itself still carries no number).

Major Arcana Attributions

The Major Arcana have their own astrological, planetary and elemental attributions; unlike the Minor Arcana, these apply to individual cards, rather than groups of cards.

CARD	ATTRIBUTION
The Fool	Air (△)
The Magician	Mercury (☿)
The High Priestess	The Moon (☽)
The Empress	Venus (♀)
The Emperor	Aries (♈)
The Pope	Taurus (♉)
The Lovers	Gemini (♊)
The Chariot	Cancer (♋)
Justice	Leo (♌)
The Hermit	Virgo (♍)
The Wheel of Fortune	Jupiter (♃)
Strength	Libra (♎)
The Hanged Man	Water (▽)
Death	Scorpio (♏)
Temperance	Sagittarius (♐)
The Devil	Capricorn (♑)
The Tower	Mars (♂)
The Star	Aquarius (♒)
The Moon	Pisces (♓)
The Sun	The Sun (☉)
Judgement	Fire (△)
The World	Saturn (♄)

CARD NUMEROLOGY

The occult significance of numbers has long been studied and it is hardly surprising to find that numerology and the tarot cross paths repeatedly.

Major Arcana Numbers

For the Major Arcana, there is a range of numerical associations which are assigned to each card.

Card Numbers

These are the numbers which appear on the face of each card and identify its place in the sequence; hence The Magician is card number 1 and Death, card number 13.

Numerical Value

This is the number used to count the cards in complex spreads. The values are assigned to each card on the basis of its astrological and elemental attribute. Thus,

* a card attributed to a Zodiac sign has a numerical value of 12

* a card attributed to a planet has a numerical value of 9

* a card attributed to an element has a numerical value of 3

Key Number

These are numbers running from 11 to 32 assigned to each card and used to position each card on The Tree of Life, the diagrammatic representation of the universe that is an essential component of the ancient Hebrew philosophical system known as the Qaballah. To underline the links between tarot and the Tree of Life, each of the Major Arcana is also assigned one of the 22 letters of the Hebrew alphabet.

It is not proposed to discuss the significance of either key numbers or the Hebrew alphabet here as this is beyond the scope of this book. However, the attributions of each to particular cards are given in the section dealing with the divinatory meanings of the arcana as a quick-reference guide or *aide-mémoire* for those who wish to pursue their study of the tarot to these more advanced planes.

Minor Arcana Numbers

For these cards, their numerical values are as follows:

★ pip cards numbered 2 to 10 in suits are assigned the face value of the particular pip (e.g. the Four of Coins has the value 4, and so on)

★ Aces are assigned the value of 5

★ Kings, Queens and Knights are each assigned the value of 4

★ Pages are assigned the value of 7

As with the numerical values of the Major Arcana, these numbers are used only for counting the cards in complicated spreads.

THE DIGNITY OF THE CARDS

Another important consideration which can influence the interpretation of a card is its dignity. Cards are considered *dignified* if the image on them appears upright when viewed by the reader and *ill-dignified* when they appear upside down and the interpretation given to each card changes with its orientation. This is in fact a relatively recent – and controversial – development in tarot divination. Some readers interpret the meaning of a reversed card as the exact opposite of an upright card, i.e. if the upright card is a positive one then its favourable elements will be lacking for the reversed card and vice-versa if the dignified card has a negative interpretation. Others simply see reversed readings as wholly negative regardless of the meaning of the upright card, so that a negative upright interpretation would be even worse when reversed. Yet other readers ignore the practice altogether, preferring to read the cards as upright, regardless as to how they are drawn from the deck. In this book, dignified and ill-dignified meanings have been given, largely following the first approach. However, to re-iterate a point made before, there are no firm rules on the subject and the aspiring reader is advised to adopt whichever system they feel most comfortable with.

However, perhaps the point deserving greatest attention when considering the dignity of cards is not the various shades of meanings of individual cards but rather how the cards relate to each other in a spread. This is because the effect of any card, whether negative or positive, can be reinforced or weakened by the cards that surround it in the spread. Therefore it is the interaction of *all* the cards in the spread and the *overall* picture they represent that is the key to a successful reading, rather than the somewhat mechanistic interpretation of individual cards. This point will be expanded in the section on doing a reading (see p.50–51).

USING THE CARDS

Over time a variety of ritual practices has grown up around using tarot cards. These vary enormously from the quasi-religious, such as burning incense and chanting invocations before a reading, to simple routines to keep your deck safe. Again, I would stress that there is no one right way of using tarot cards. Experiment with whichever particular rituals you feel comfortable with: an open mind and personal experience will reveal those which produce the best results for you. The routines explained below amount to the minimum 'best practice' that I recommend you adopt.

CHOOSING YOUR DECK

Intuition is one of the keys to making progress with the tarot and you should begin to develop this faculty from the very moment you choose your first working deck. There is a quite bewildering array of different decks to choose from and to the novice, one deck may appear to be as good as another. This is not the case: it is important to choose a deck that you feel entirely comfortable with because you will be more attuned to the myriad interpretations that your spreads produce if the symbolism and imagery used on your cards appeal *instinctively* to you. Simply put, you will do better readings if your cards arouse your imagination and stimulate your unconscious mind. Therefore, you should take your time and choose your deck with care. Ideally, you should try to see a selection of cards from any deck before you buy it.

While there is now probably a deck to suit every personal taste, there is a case to be made that newcomers to tarot should confine themselves to one of the traditional decks, such as the Tarot de Marseilles, the Rider-Waite or the Morgan Greer. The reason for this is simple: the books which most novices will be consulting tend to use these decks or others with imagery derived from them and it undoubtedly simplifies the learning process if the imagery on your own deck corresponds directly with that in the books you are using.

Many larger bookshops now stock tarot decks but if you are having difficulty in obtaining a set you like or would simply like to see a wider range, a number of card suppliers is given on p.252.

KEEPING AND HANDLING YOUR CARDS

Having chosen your deck, there are a number of

practices which you should follow in order to get the best from your cards.

Storage

When not in use, your cards should be kept wrapped in a scarf or similar piece of cloth. Traditionally, this should be made of silk whose natural fibres are believed to prevent the cards from becoming contaminated by 'vibrations' or 'impressions' from their surroundings which may adversely affect the accuracy of any reading using them. The silk can be any colour you wish, although many readers insist on a rich self-colour, such as purple, royal blue or gold. As a further protection from surrounding negative influences, the silk-wrapped cards should be stored in a wooden box.

Whether you accept the eso-teric explana-tions behind this practice is a matter of p e r s o n a l preference.

However, keeping your cards in this fashion does have the practical benefit of reducing everyday wear-and-tear, and it also keeps them away from prying hands. By their very nature, tarot decks are often attractive but for the reasons outlined in the next section, it is important that you keep your cards out of others' idly curious hands.

'Breaking in' Your Deck

Once you have your deck, handle the cards as often as possible. Not only will this make you familiar with the design and feel of the images used on each card, but more importantly, it will help impregnate your deck with your own vibrations. This 'breaking in' (which is sometimes also called 'seasoning' or 'working up') of a new deck has been likened to breaking in a new pair of shoes: they may look like hundreds of other similar pairs but by wearing them you mould them to fit the unique contours of your feet. So it is with tarot cards; through repeated handling, the deck absorbs the psychic vibrations of its owner and so becomes personalised to her or him. This is an important process because it is easier to develop your own psychic skills and intuition using a deck seasoned by you, rather than one contaminated by someone else's vibrations. For this reason, never use another person's deck and except when you are reading, ***never let anyone else handle your cards***.

PREPARING FOR A READING

An essential ingredient of a good reading is an atmosphere which allows both the reader and the Querant to remain focused. Therefore, wherever possible you should manipulate your surroundings to minimise the number of possible distractions:

* read the cards with only the Querant present

* read the cards on a small table that you can use exclusively for this purpose

* keep background 'noise' to a minimum (i.e. no television or radio)

* adjust the lighting in the room so that the reading table is emphasised; candles placed close to the table are useful for this.

It is also important that both you and the Querant are relaxed so it is vital that your approach and manner remains calm and easy – too much mystique can set some people on edge!

However, a word of caution: once people learn of your interest in tarot, you can sometimes find yourself being pressurised into performing your 'party piece' by doing a reading before a crowd at a party or other social event. Wherever possible you should try to avoid this; it's unlikely that a good reading will result and you can leave yourself open to ridicule.

Once you have your surroundings prepared, cover the table with your reading cloth, another large piece of silk, and take the cards from their wrapping. You are now ready to begin the reading.

CHOOSING WHICH SPREAD TO USE

Your first step should be to ask the Querant to formulate in their own mind any particular question that they wished answered or an area of their life that they wish advice on. Depending on the information being sought, an appropriate spread should be chosen.

Simpler Spreads

Smaller spreads, using only a limited number of cards, are best for:

* answering specific questions such as those requiring a straight 'yes' or 'no' answer

* examining a specifc area of the Querant's life

* examining a specific difficulty that the Querant is seeking advice on

Complex Spreads

More complex spreads which present different areas of the Querant's life should be used for:

* an overview of the Querant's life, and the circumstances and the influences operating on it

It is important that you are well-versed in whatever spread you select. If you are a novice, it is best to stick to the simpler spreads until you have built up sufficient experience and knowledge to allow you to handle more complex spreads and interpretations. Various spreads are described from p.60 onwards.

SHUFFLING AND SELECTING THE CARDS

Shuffling

Having decided which spread you will be using, you should then select a Significator (if you decide to use one), using your preferred method (see p.28). The selected card is removed from the deck before shuffling and placed face up on the table to act as a focus for you.

You should shuffle the cards well, making sure not to correct the orientation of any of them if you intend to give reversed interpretations. The Querant should then shuffle the cards briefly before placing them face down on the table. If reversed interpretations are to be a feature of the reading, it is vital that you pay particular attention to the orientation of the deck while the Querant is shuffling it: when you come to deal the cards, they should be dignified to you as they were to the Querant, in other words, the bottom edge of the deck closest to the Querant should be likewise to you.

Selecting
There are a number of different methods of selecting the cards to be used in the spread, most of which are variants of the following:

Cutting the Deck
* the Querant cuts the deck twice using their left hand (which is believed to be closer to the heart and so to the true nature of a person)

* the first cut is placed to the left of the remains of the original stack and this process is repeated on the first cut to give three piles of cards

Cutting the deck

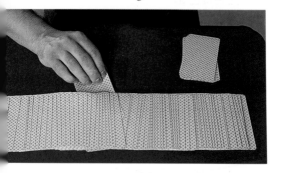

Fanning the deck

* the deck is then reassembled in the same order (i.e. right to left), so that the remains of the original stack are placed on top of the first cut which is then placed on top of the second.

* the required number of cards can now be dealt from the top of the reassembled deck

Fanning the Deck

* the entire deck is fanned out in a line face down on the table

* the Querant then chooses the appropriate number of cards.

* the reader should note the sequence in which the cards are chosen as this will determine the order in which they are subsequently laid out: the first card chosen is placed in position 1 of the spread, the second in position 2, and so on.

LAYING OUT THE CARDS

The selected cards are dealt from the top of the pile and placed face down on the table in the pattern of the spread. When revealing the face of the cards, it is essential that you never flip the cards up and over as you would, say, when turning a calendar page. Rather, the cards are turned over side-to-side, as if turning the page of a book so as to preserve their particular dignity. The orientation is decided from the viewpoint of the reader, rather than the Querant. When all the cards have been turned face up, you can begin your interpretation.

Cards should be turned from side-to-side in order to preserve their dignity

INTERPRETING THE SPREAD

This is the point where all your rehearsing, knowledge and experience comes into play, the point where you must interpret through the cards someone's life and the influences on it. Of course, if you are a novice and have only limited knowledge and experience, then it can be a terrifying moment, particularly if you are facing a Querant for your first 'live' reading. Practice is the key and there is, unfortunately, no substitute for it; it is only by doing readings repeatedly that the associations start to be made, that you start to see connections and make the intuitive leaps between apparently unrelated experiences which are the hallmark of the experienced reader. That being so, however, there are a number of techniques which can be learned swiftly that will hone your interpretive skills and greatly improve the ease and smoothness of your reading.

Keep It Simple

It may seem obvious to say it but work within your capabilities, particularly if reading for other people. When starting out, concentrate on learning only a few straightforward spreads very well and only move onto more complex ones when you feel you are completely comfortable with them.

Interpret the Spread as a Whole

Since it is usual to learn the meaning of the cards in isolation from each other, there is a not unnatural tendency for new readers to focus too heavily upon interpretations of individual cards in a spread. Unfortunately, this tends to make readings rather mechanistic and unpersonal, and often gives the feeling that it is an exercise being done by rote. Remember that the spread is greater than the sum of its parts: the cards should not be interpreted solely in isolation but how they interact with each other to give a unified picture of the Querant's life rather than a series of random snapshots of it.

Look for the Overall Theme of the Spread

Check for the predominance of certain types or combinations of cards to get an overall picture of the spread. For example,

* a predominance of particular Minor Arcana suits means that the life experience attribution of the particular suit (see p.24) will be a major theme of the reading. For example, a preponderance of Wands means that the Querant's career will feature strongly, as will his or her emotional life if many Cups are present

Many Wands	*means*	**Career**
Many Cups	*means*	**Emotions**
Many Swords	*means*	**Intellectual activity**
Many Coins	*means*	**Material affairs**

* many Major Arcana cards means that the Querant will be experiencing important changes in his life which go to the very core of his being and beliefs, changes that are often beyond the Querant's direct control

* many court cards suggests that there are many outside influences operating in the Querant's

life and that the actions of other people will be a governing factor

* many reversed cards (if you are using them) point to obstacles, delays and difficulties in general for the Querant

Consider the Specific Meanings of the Cards

Having formed a general impression of what the cards are saying, use this overview as a point of reference for a more detailed examination of the cards as they relate to their specfic positions in the spread. This can be done either by interpreting each card in sequence or by focusing in on specific cards which pick up on a major theme of the spread and using this as the key interpretation to which all the other cards relate. This latter approach is usually only attempted by more experienced readers. Whichever approach you choose (and depending on the spread you are using), pay particular attention to certain areas of the spread and how the meanings of the cards relate to one another:

* examine areas of the spread concerning the Querant's past and future. Are there influences and actions from the former which have a bearing on the latter? Will these improve or worsen the Querant's situation?

* examine those areas of the Querant's life where major difficulties are being experienced and try to discern the likely causes and outcomes

* examine areas of the spread showing possible outcomes. How do these tie in with the other individual interpretations?

Drawing threads through different areas of the spread such as these and then pulling the various meanings together into a coherent 'story' is a skill only achieved through experience but reaching this level is something all novice readers should aspire to.

Combinations of Cards

While considering the meanings of the cards as they have fallen in the spread, be sure to look not only at the individual card in its position but also on the cards immediately surrounding it.

Some tarot writers provide long lists of specific meanings ascribed to combinations of one particular card falling next to another. Personally, I think that such rigid interpretations can be overstressed and become too prescriptive and limiting for the reader. I would go no further than suggest learning the combinations on the following list which gives the meanings traditionally ascribed to multiples of cards of the same face appearing within a spread.

CARD	MULTIPLE	MEANING
King	4	Important meetings
	3	High status; honours granted
	2	Business opportunities
Queen	4	Arguments
	3	Influential women
	2	Slander or maliciousness
Knight	4	Swiftness; a dominant clique
	3	Unexpected meetings
	2	Friends from the past
Page	4	New plans or ideas
	3	Groups of young people
	2	Fun and enjoyment
Ten	4	Responsibility and anxiety
	3	Commercial transactions
Nine	4	Extra responsibilities
	3	Correspondence
Eight	4	Lots of news simultaneously
	3	Extensive travelling

CARD	MULTIPLE	MEANING
Seven	4	Disappointments
	3	Contracts and alliances
Six	4	Pleasure and contentment
	3	Achievements and successes
Five	4	Order and consistency
	3	Disputes and quarrels
Four	4	Peace and quiet
	3	Much effort
Three	4	Decision and resolution
	3	Deceit
Two	4	Conversations; conferences
	3	Reorganisation
Ace	4	Powerful forces at work
	3	Success and wealth
	2	New workplace or home

Polarity of Suits

However, there is one aspect of card combinations that you should be aware of, namely the polarity of suits, which is determined by their governing element:

> **Wands (Fire)** *are opposite to* **Cups (Water)**
>
> **Swords (Air)** *are opposite to* **Coins (Earth)**

The effect of this is that the meaning of an individual card will be modified depending on the cards adjacent to it:

★ a card's meaning will be *reinforced* if the adjacent cards are of its own suit

★ a card's meaning will be *weakened* if the adjacent cards are of the opposite suit

★ where a card falls between others from either one or both of the suits that it is *not* opposite to (e.g. a Wand between a Sword and a Coin, or between two Coins), then the effect on the central card is generally supportive (although not as much as it would be if it falls between two cards of its own suit)

* Major Arcana cards flanked by Minor Arcana cards of the same suit will be strongly affected, positvely or negatively, by the meaning and dignity of the lesser cards

* cards of opposite suits surrounding a cental card tend to neutralise the influence each may have brought to bear and so the central card should be read without modification

Consider a Card's Various Interpretations

Unless you are very fortunate, there will always be one or two cards in every spread which will defy your initial attempts to make them conform to your overview or produce sensible links with the surrounding cards. When this happens, consider any alternative or secondary meanings they may have to see if these are better suited to making the card fit in more with the spread overview. Remember that you are trying to provide the Querant with an ordered and consistent 'story' from the spread, rather than a disparate collecton of conflicting interpretations. At the very least, trust your intuition!

Summarise Your Reading

At the end of a reading, it is good practice to summarise the various points that you have touched in the course of the reading (for both you and the Querant).

SOME WORDS OF ADVICE

Never forget that you are taking on an important responsibility when you agree to read the cards for another person and so you should be aware of the implications this can have for both you and the Querant.

* at all times, be professional in your attitude and conduct (even if you are not reading for payment). It is an essential part of a good reading that your actions are smooth, confident and well-rehearsed. If Querants believe they are dealing with someone who takes tarot seriously, then they themselves are likely to be in a more positive frame of mind

* avoid an overly theatrical, or overly mystical presentation. This may make some people edgy or leave others feeling that the whole process is ridiculous. Either way, they won't be relaxed and a good reading will be difficult to achieve

* Remember that even the most sceptical of Querants can prove surprisingly receptive to what he or she is being told, so be responsible at all times in terms of what you say. Be aware of the Querant's reactions to what you are saying and be prepared to change tack if there is anything that appears to be unsettling or upsetting them

* In particular, take great care when interpreting a strongly negative spread. Try to tone down its blacker aspects (if only to give the Querant some hope for the future) and *never* make predictions of death, serious illness or personal catastrophe

SPREADS

This chapter contains a variety of spreads which will allow you to put into practice all that you have learned to date.

3-CARD SPREAD

◆

PREFERRED USE
To help understand and clarify available options before taking action to solve a particular problem

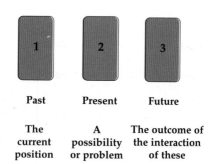

	1	2	3
	Past	**Present**	**Future**
OR	The current position	A possibility or problem	The outcome of the interaction of these

◆ What the Spread Reveals ◆

This is a simple but very useful spread that can have a wide variety of meanings assigned to each of the positions by the reader. The following are two of my favourites but you can add your own as you wish.

1st Card: The Past Shows the Querant's past experiences which may cast some light on the present problem.

2nd Card: The Present Reveals what the Querant is feeling at the moment.

3rd Card: The Future Shows the result of the course of action the Querant takes.

Alternatively,

1st Card: The Current Position Shows an overview of the Querant's present situation.

2nd Card: A Possibility or Problem Identifies a new set of circumstances about to act upon the Querant; the forces driving these may be positive or negative.

3rd Card: The Outcome Reveals the effect of the new circumstances on the Querant.

7-CARD HORSESHOE SPREAD

◆

PREFERRED USE

To give guidance on a specific problem when the Querant is unsure of the best course to follow

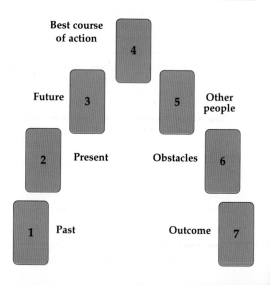

Best course of action — 4

Future — 3

Other people — 5

Present — 2

Obstacles — 6

Past — 1

Outcome — 7

✦ WHAT THE SPREAD REVEALS ✦

1st Card: The Past Reveals something specific in the Querant's past relating to the present problem. Suggests referral to past experiences to avoid repeating past mistakes or to employ previously successful tactics once more.

2nd Card: The Present May elucidate the Querant's problem. Compare with cards 1 and 3 to see whether circumstance improve or deteriorate.

3rd Card: The Future Shows the result of the course of action the Querant takes (see Card 7).

4th Card: Best Course of Action Indicates what should be done to resolve the Querant's problem. Compare with cards 3 and 7 to see whether this advice is going to be followed.

5th Card: Other People Shows how other people feature in the Querant's problem. Can indicate how others around the Querant are behaving or feel about what is happening. If other people are the problem, this card may indicate something about their role.

6th Card: Obstacles Reveals obstacles to resolving the problem, in some cases not always negative elements; positive behaviour or feelings may not always be appropriate when resolving the problem.

7th Card: The Outcome Shows the course of action the Querant is likely to take and their feelings.

6-CARD SPREAD

◆

PREFERRED USE

To obtain a broad overview of those areas of the Querant's life that are of special interest to him

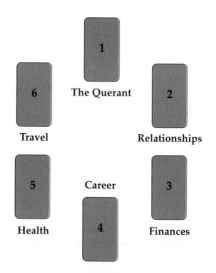

◆ What the Spread Reveals ◆

The card positions in this spread can represent any area that the Querant is seeking advice on and you should agree in advance what the six categories are to be. Those listed below represent the broad range of areas that most people are interested in.

1st Card: The Querant Reveals something about the Querant himself that is presently an important factor in his life. The interpretations of the other cards should be grounded on this one to reveal the possible source of this condition and any likely changes in it.

2nd Card: Relationships Shows the state of the Querant's relationships with people around him. This is broader than simply a reflection of his love life and should encompass all his personal interactions.

3rd Card: Finances Shows the state of the Querant's finances.

4th Card: Career Indicates the Querant's current position at work and his feelings towards it.

5th Card: Health Usually this will relate to the Querant's health but may refer to that of someone else close to him.

6th Card: Travel Reveals whether the Querant is likely to be travelling in the near future, and the extent and nature of any trips. It may also point to others travelling to meet the Querant.

YES/NO SPREAD

◆

> **PREFERRED USE**
> To answer a question which requires a simple
> 'yes' or 'no' answer

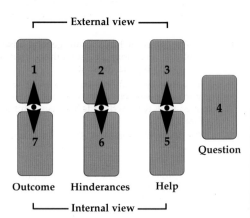

✦ What the Spread Reveals ✦

For this spread, the question should be phrased so that a 'yes' answer is regarded as something positive for the Querant, and the 'no' as something negative. Generally, if 4 or more of the cards are upright the answer will be 'yes', and if 4 or more are reversed then the answer will be 'no', although the cards' specific meaning will still have to be analysed.

4th Card: The Question Indicates the general subject matter of the question, i.e. something that is presently concerning the Querant.

3rd & 5th Cards: Helpful Influences Reveal factors that contribute positively to the Querant achieving her desired goal. Reversed cards here can point to a lack of assistance.

2nd & 6th Cards: Hinderances Shows those factors, sometimes hidden, that are operating against the Querant's interests.

1st & 7th Cards: Outcomes Shows the outcome, perhaps an event and an indication of how the Querant feels about it.

Cards 1, 2 and 3 can be further interpreted as indicators of the Querant's life and personality as viewed by others, and contrasted to Cards 5, 6 and 7, which represent the Querant's views on events.

QUESTION AND ANSWER SPREAD

◆

PREFERRED USE

For any question that can be answered in terms of
a straightforward 'yes' or 'no'

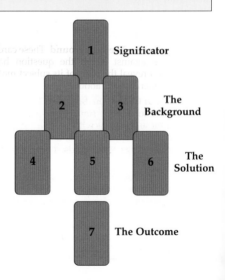

1 Significator

2   **3**   The
         Background

4   **5**   **6**   The
                  Solution

7 The Outcome

◆ What the Spread Reveals ◆

The Querant should identify her question in advance of the spread beginning; it should be phrased so that a 'yes' answer is regraded as something positive for the Querant, and the 'no' as something negative.

1st Card: Significator This is chosen to represent the Querant, as outlined on p.28.

2nd & 3rd Cards: The Background These cards show the setting against which the question has been framed and reveal the roots of its subject matter and how the Querant feels about it.

4th, 5th & 6th Cards: The Solution These cards give the answer to the question. A majority of reversed cards in these positions will generally suggest a 'no' answer and of upright cards, a 'yes', although the specific meanings of the cards should also be taken into account.

7th Card: The Outcome Reveals the final outcome. If Cards 4, 5 and 6 suggest a 'no' answer, then this card will suggest a way forward from the disappointment, possibly with a view to ultimately achieving the desired goal. If the answer has been 'yes', this will indicate the effect that this will have on the Querant's life.

7-CARD INFINITY SPREAD

◆

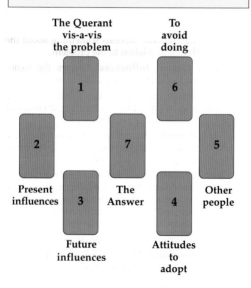

The Querant
vis-a-vis
the problem

To
avoid
doing

1

6

Present
influences

2

7

5

Other
people

3

The
Answer

4

Future
influences

Attitudes
to
adopt

◆ What the Spread Reveals ◆

This spread can be done either with just the 22 Major Arcana cards or the whole deck. In general, the nature and importance of the problem on which the Querant is seeking guidance should let you decide which approach to adopt: the weightier the problem, the more you should consider using only the Major Arcana cards.

1st Card: The Querant Reveals something about the Querant himself in relation to the problem.

2nd Card: Present Influences Shows the major influences in the Querant's life at this time.

3rd Card: Future Influences Reveals those factors that will be brought to bear on the Querant before a solution is found to the problem.

4th Card: Attitudes to Adopt Indicates the best frame of mind for the Querant to adopt in order to deal with the problem effectively.

5th Card: Other People Shows how other people feature in the Querant's problem. Can indicate how others around the Querant are behaving or feel about what is happening. If other people are the problem, this may indicate something about their role.

6th Card: To Avoid Offers advice on attitudes, areas or people to avoid when dealing with the problem.

7th Card: The Answer The solution.

21-CARD SPREAD

◆

PREFERRED USE

To provide a general overview of the Querant's life and the forces acting on it.

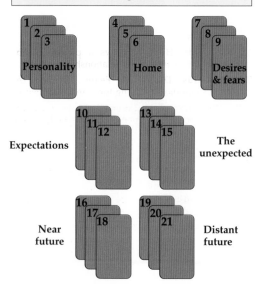

✦ What the Spread Reveals ✦

This is a relatively complicated spread to interpret since each position has three cards. Try to present a coherent interpretation of each group of cards, even when sometimes they individually may seem at odds with one another.

1st-3rd Cards: Personality Reveals aspects of the Querant herself.

4th-6th Cards: Home Shows a picture of the Querant's home life and her relationships within it.

7th-9th Cards: Desires & Fears Reveals the Querant's ambitions, driving force and nightmares.

10th-12th Cards: Expectations Indicates what the Querant expects to happen, either a specific event, or a course of action.

13th-15th Cards: The Unexpected Shows an unforeseen obstacle or an alternative course of action to be taken by the Querant. Compare this with Cards 10–12.

16th-18th Cards: Near Future Reveals likely events or outcomes due to take place soon.

19th-21st Cards: Distant Future Shows longer-term developments. Compare this with Cards 16–18 to see if the situation improves or deteriorates.

CHOICES SPREAD

◆

PREFERRED USE

To give guidance on a specific course to follow
when two alternative options are open

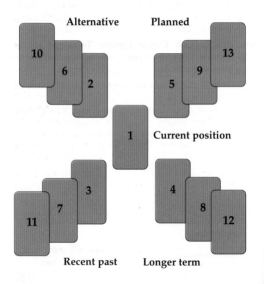

Alternative   Planned

Current position

Recent past   Longer term

◆ What the Spread Reveals ◆

This is a useful spread to consult when you have already framed a solution to a problem in your mind but would like to explore the possible outcome of an alternative approach.

1st Card: Current position Reveals a general view of the situation facing the Querant, perhaps highlighting a specific aspect of it that merits particular attention.

4th, 8th & 12th Cards: Longer Term Influences Reveals the circumstances which have given rise to the problem now confronting the Querant

3rd, 7th & 11th Cards: Recent Past Influences Highlights specific events or forces in the recent past which have helped shape the problem in its present form. There might also be a suggestion of the different options being considered or of the motivations behind them. These cards should be compared and contrasted with Cards 4, 8 and 12.

5th, 9th & 13th Cards: The Planned Outcome Indicates the likely outcomes if the Querant pursues her planned course of action.

2nd, 6th & 10th Cards: The Alternative Outcome Indicates the likely outcomes if the alternative solution is tried.

Comparing the last two interpretations will show which option will produce the most favourable solution.

ALCHEMIST'S SPREAD

◆

> **PREFERRED USE**
> This spread should be drawn only once for each Querant during his or her lifetime

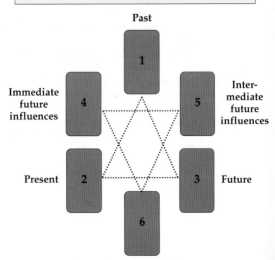

Past

Immediate future influences

Inter-mediate future influences

Present

Future

Long-term future influences

◆ WHAT THE SPREAD REVEALS ◆

This is a spread of some antiquity, reputedly dating back to the late Middle Ages. As befitting a spread that is claimed to have been devised by Nostradamus, it has deeply mystical overtones.

1st Card: The Past Represents the sum total of the Querant's past life experience.

2nd Card: The Present Represents all that the Querant will achieve in this life.

3rd Card: The Future Indicates the Querant's final position on the Wheel of Life.

4th Card: Immediate future influences Indicates those influences that will occur in the Querant's life in the very near future.

5th Card: Intermediate future influences Indicates those influences that will occur in the Querant's life in the next few years or so.

6th Card: Long-term future influences Indicates those influences that will come to bear at the end of the Querant's life.

CELTIC CROSS SPREAD

◆

| **PREFERRED USE** |
| To give guidance on a specific problem |

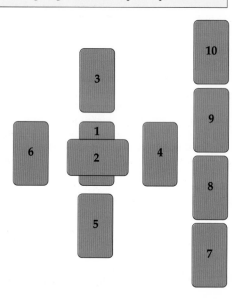

◆ WHAT THE SPREAD REVEALS ◆

This is perhaps the most written about spread of all, and although so popular, it is be one which can be quite difficult for novices to master. Unusually, it is laid out in two separate steps: cards 1–6 which are then interpreted, and then cards 7–10 which are read in turn.

1st Card: Current Influences Reveals the influences operating on the Querant and shows the direction of the reading generally.

2nd Card: Obstacles Shows the nature of the obstacles immediately before the Querant.

3rd Card: Specific Goals Shows the desired aims of the Querant and also the best that is likely to be achieved under the current conditions.

4th Card: Past Foundations Indicates the events or influences in the distant past from which the Querant's current situation has arisen.

5th Card: Past Events Shows a more recent influence which is in the process of waning.

6th Card: Future Influences Reveals a new influence that will soon be brought to bear on the Querant's life.

7th Card: The Querant Provides further information about the Querant and how she feels about or relates to her current environment.

8th Card: Home & Environment   Reveals the Querant's influence on the people around her and how she fits into her home and work surroundings.

9th Card: Inner Emotions   Indicates the Querant's hopes and fears.

10th Card: Final Result   Shows the final outcome, the product of all the other influences revealed elsewhere in the spread.

THE MEANING OF THE CARDS

This chapter provides the meanings that are given individually to each of the 78 cards in the deck.

The Major Arcana cards are dealt with first and then each of the Minor Arcana suits follow. For each card, dignified and ill-dignified meanings (see p.36) are given, as are its astrological and numerical attributions (see pp.24 and 34). Note that certain of these attributions will only be used by more experienced readers but they are included here as an *aide-mémoire*. Also included for quick reference and ease-of-learning are, the key themes of each reversed and upright interpretation.

I would like to explain my use of the personal pronoun in the pages which follow: solely for ease of reading, I alternate references to the gender of Querants and readers on successive pages, rather than resort to the gramatically clumsy 'his or her' or 's/he'. So, if the Querant in a particular card is referred to as being specifically male or female, please interpret and change this according to your own gender.

THE FOOL

THE FOOL

Attributions

Card Number   0
Astrological Ruler   Air   △
Key Number   11
Numerical Value   3
Hebrew Letter   Aleph   א

✦ Interpretations ✦

Dignified

Upright, The Fool represents a new beginning, a fresh start in any aspect of the Querant's life, the position in the spread indicating which. She will be faced with important choices and decisions needing to be made as she begins this new life-cycle which may not have been planned, and there will be difficult challenges ahead involving a degree of risk. However, if the Querant approaches these with energy and optimism, a positive outcome is indicated.

KEY THEMES
fresh starts • important decisions • optimism

Ill-dignified

Reversed, The Fool gives a clear warning that the Querant must resist the temptation to act recklessly or immaturely in any new situation facing them, perhaps through an unwillingness to accept responsibility or commitments. Due consideration is required but instead problems and indiscretion resulting from impatience or impulsiveness are indicated.

KEY THEMES
recklessness • immaturity • lack of commitment

THE MAGICIAN

THE MAGICIAN

Attributions

Card Number	1
Astrological Ruler	Mercury ☿
Key Number	12
Numerical Value	9
Hebrew Letter	Beth ב

◆ INTERPRETATIONS ◆

Dignified

This card signifies that the Querant is an intelligent and skilful communicator and possesses the self-confidence and drive to translate ideas into productive action. These talents should be used in a new opportunity presenting itself in a practical rather than a theoretical sphere, most likely in business or politics. It may be a risky venture but the Querant's strength of will and ability to channel his energies into achieving desired results will ensure success.

KEY THEMES

confidence • good communications • practical skill

Ill-dignified

The reversed Magician signifies that the Querant lacks confidence, possibly arising from shyness or a poor self-image, and is prone to indecision and hesitation. Another interpretation is that the positive aspects of the card may be being used to achieve selfish or dishonest goals or that others around the Querant may not be all that they seem.

KEY THEMES

hesitancy • lack of confidence • dishonesty

THE HIGH PRIESTESS

Attributions

Card Number	2
Astrological Ruler	Moon ☽
Key Number	13
Numerical Value	9
Hebrew Letter	Gimel ℷ

◆ Interpretations ◆

Dignified

Good judgement and self-reliance are indicated by The High Priestess' appearance and for the Querant, the heart rather than the head – intuition rather than reason – should be the guide in making an important decision. Yet depending on the spread, this guidance may in fact derive from another person who is going to assist the Querant. The card can also point to something hidden, facts or influences, affecting the Querant's current state with its position in the spread indicating the likely area of her life affected.

KEY THEMES
foresight • understanding • inner wisdom

Ill-dignified

When reversed, this card points to a lack of inner knowledge and problems arising from a failure to follow paths one knows intuitively to be right. In some circumstances, this may lead to unfulfilled potential or suppressed emotions.

KEY THEMES
potential denied • lack of foresight

THE EMPRESS

Attributions

Card Number	3
Astrological Ruler	Venus ♀
Key Number	14
Numerical Value	9
Hebrew Letter	Daleth ד

✦ Interpretations ✦

Dignified

An excellent card to find in a spread. It signifies a harmony and satisfaction for the Querant in many aspects of her life, particularly those relating to physical and emotional well-being: families, relationships, the home. Maternal influences are strongly indicated and the card may point to the birth of a child (not necessarily that of the Querant directly), or indeed to a successful marriage. A powerful flow of artistic creativity and inspiration are also suggested.

KEY THEMES

fulfilment • well-being • creative abundance

Ill-dignified

The reversed Empress signifies problems with the Querant's physical or emotional well-being, possibly leading to, or arising from, insecurity and self-doubt. Conflicts between the sexes are highlighted generally with domestic difficulties and particularly, problems relating to fertility and pregnancy are indicated. The urge to create may also be being suppressed.

KEY THEMES

insecurity • domestic disturbances

THE EMPEROR

THE EMPEROR

Attributions

Card Number	4
Astrological Ruler	Aries ♈
Key Number	15
Numerical Value	12
Hebrew Letter	Heh ה

◆ INTERPRETATIONS ◆

Dignified

This card can signify a very powerful male influence in the Querant's life, one involving leadership and authority; it may be the Querant himself, or a person or institution around them. As indicative of qualities, The Emperor represents self-discipline, organisation, stability and action as the path to fulfilment. In some spreads, it can be a good indicator of promotion or a move to a new position of responsibility and respect, one in which these qualities can be exercised.

KEY THEMES
male influences • authority • rationality

Ill-dignified

Reversed, The Emperor points to problems with authority particularly involving a dominant male figure – perhaps a father or partner or boss. The Querant may be resentful and rebellious because he feels he is being denied responsibility by others, but the card can also signify some immaturity leading to a shirking of responsibility.

KEY THEMES
rebelliousness • immaturity

THE POPE

Attributions

Card Number	5
Astrological Ruler	Taurus ♉
Key Number	16
Numerical Value	12
Hebrew Letter	Vau ו

✦ INTERPRETATIONS ✦

Dignified

This card has two main interpretations. One is that it signifies advice and guidance from a professional source – teacher, lawyer, spiritual adviser, etc. – either being sought by the Querant or offered by her in one of these capacities. The other is that The Pope represents orthodoxy and conformity in the Querant's life, and indicates that observation of the moral, religious or social conventions of her culture will bring them greatest fulfilment.

KEY THEMES
conformity • good counsel

Ill-dignified

In a reversed position, The Pope signifies non-conformity and urges the Querant to consider less obvious and less orthodox approaches to resolve a current problem, as conventional, tried-and-tested paths may not offer success. It also warns that any advice sought may be untrustworthy or ill-matched to the Querant's true needs.

KEY THEMES
unconventionality • misleading advice

THE LOVERS

Attributions

Card Number	6
Astrological Ruler	Gemini ♊
Key Number	17
Numerical Value	12
Hebrew Letter	Zain ז

◆ INTERPRETATIONS ◆

Dignified

On a simple level, this card may be seen to represent love (possibly rekindled) and happy relationships. At a deeper level, The Lovers signifies an important choice to be made in some sphere of the Querant's life, one for which there are several – often conflicting – options to be weighed up. This is clearly worrying the Querant but this card, upright, indicates that due consideration will resolve any internal struggles and lead ultimately to the corrrect decision.

KEY THEMES
relationships • conflicting choices

Ill-dignified

Ill-dignified, this card warns of rash decisions that are likely to be subsequently regretted. The Querant is being urged to consider carefully all the factors before her. It also warns against indecision and/or inconsistency: the Querant must choose a path carefully and adhere to it. In relationships, the reversed Lovers indicates frustrations and mistiming.

KEY THEMES
ill-considered choices • frustration

THE CHARIOT

Attributions

Card Number	7
Astrological Ruler	Cancer ♋
Key Number	18
Numerical Value	12
Hebrew Letter	Cheth ח

✦ INTERPRETATIONS ✦

Dignified

The Chariot indicates a period of intense hard work, an uphill struggle against setbacks and problems. The time scale is fluid: it may belong to the past, the present, or the near future but with the card upright, a good outcome is assured. This will be the result of the character traits signified by The Chariot: confidence, strength of purpose, organisational ability and endurance. Harnessing these in pursuit of the Querant's goal will overcome all obstacles.

KEY THEMES

effort leading to success • strength of character

Ill-dignified

The reversed Chariot also points to a period of effort and challenge but with a less assured outcome for the Querant. The character traits signified by the upright card may be lacking and indicates the Querant's loss of control over the events in their life as a result. This in turn can lead to feelings of frustration, anger and powerlessness.

KEY THEMES

loss of control • unresolved difficulties

JUSTICE

Attributions

Card Number	8
Astrological Ruler	Leo ♌
Key Number	19
Numerical Value	12
Hebrew Letter	Teth ט

◆ INTERPRETATIONS ◆

Dignified

On a practical level, this card signifies justice and fair treatment for the Querant, not only in legal entanglements but in any sphere where judgements are to be made or disputes resolved. If a legal judgement is awaited, then this card indicates it will likely be in the Querant's favour. On another level, it urges the Querant to seek an equilibrium between opposing forces in his life, material and spiritual, physical and mental, rational and intuitive.

KEY THEMES
justice • balance

Ill-dignified

Even in its reversed aspect, the card signifies that justice will still be done in the legal arena – only now this means a judgement will rightly go against the Querant. However, with this orientation the card also suggests unfairness, bias and misjudgement, with the Querant as either the perpetrator or the victim of this.

KEY THEMES
adverse legal decisions • injustice • bias

THE HERMIT

THE HERMIT

Attributions

Card Number	9
Astrological Ruler	Virgo ♍
Key Number	20
Numerical Value	12
Hebrew Letter	Yod ׳

✦ INTERPRETATIONS ✦

Dignified

This card stresses the need for the Querant to stand back from a situation, even removing themselves physically from it, so as to evaluate their circumstances. As an extension of this, it also indicates the need for a period of quiet inner reflection, where the Querant will be able to assess her true needs and aims, free from everday pressures. By searching deep within herself in this way, the Querant will find the solutions to long-term directions in life or to more immediate difficulties.

KEY THEMES
introspection • solitude

Ill-dignified

Self-reliance is a positive force under the upright card but reversed is now a negative influence. It indicates that the Querant has rejected help or advice (particularly from family or friends) and is now struggling. There may be feelings of isolation and loneliness as a result, or an obstinate resistance to necessary change.

KEY THEMES
isolation • obstinacy

THE WHEEL OF FORTUNE

Attributions

Card Number	10
Astrological Ruler	Jupiter ♃
Key Number	21
Numerical Value	9
Hebrew Letter	Kaph כ

✦ INTERPRETATIONS ✦

Dignified

A generally optimistic card. The upright Wheel of Fortune signifies the end of one cycle in the Querant's life and the start of a new one. Often this will be the result of events or circumstances outwith the Querant's control but the changes will nevertheless be positive. The position of the card in the spread is important in indicating particular areas of the Querant's life where these changes will have the greatest impact.

KEY THEMES
cyclical change • good fortune

Ill-dignified

Reversed, this card signifies the downward turn of the wheel and the start of a negative phase for the Querant. Again, the catalyst for this change may be uncontrollable or unexpected and once more, the other cards can shed light on particular aspects of, or influences on, these difficulties. Yet the wheel will continue to turn and this period will end.

KEY THEMES
unexpected difficulties

STRENGTH

Attributions

Card Number   11
Astrological Ruler   Libra ♎
Key Number   22
Numerical Value   12
Hebrew Letter   Lamed ל

◆ INTERPRETATIONS ◆

Dignified

An extremely powerful card, Strength signifies the Querant's ability to cope with, and overcome, his problems by facing up to them with courage, determination and perseverance, rather than trying to avoid them. The Querant is also urged to control negative impulses such as jealousy, anger and spite, and instead to direct this emotional energy into more positive expressions in order to overcome obstacles to happiness and fulfilment. On another level, the recovery of health and well-being is indicated.

KEY THEMES
confronting problems • strength of will

Ill-dignified

Reversed, this card signifies a surrender to base emotions together with a self-indulgence and misdirection of inner energies which weakens the Querant's ability to cope with a difficult situation. It indicates a lack of self-discipline and a corresponding loss of belief in one's own abilities.

KEY THEMES
misdirection of inner energy • poor self-control

THE HANGED MAN

Attributions

Card Number	12
Astrological Ruler	Water ▽
Key Number	23
Numerical Value	3
Hebrew Letter	Mem מ

✦ Interpretations ✦

Dignified

Two major indications of this upright card are change and sacrifice. The Querant faces a turning point in her life, one offering different paths to follow. Difficult but necessary sacrifices will be made in pursuing the elected route, although others may not understand this. The sacrifices may be material or may involve abandoning a former viewpoint, but whatever their nature, they will ultimately lead to a new sense of spirituality and emotional fulfilment.

KEY THEMES
transition • sacrifice leading to attainment

Ill-dignified

The reversed card warns against pursuing purely material or egotistical goals to the detriment of one's spiritual needs. Stagnation and a lack of growth are signified, with the Querant lacking any sense of a higher purpose to life and, consequently, being deeply unhappy. A re-ordering of priorities is needed but this may be being resisted.

KEY THEMES
personal stagnation • resistance to change

DEATH

Attributions

Card Number	13
Astrological Ruler	Scorpio ♏
Key Number	24
Numerical Value	12
Hebrew Letter	Nun ﬍

◆ INTERPRETATIONS ◆

Dignified

Upright, this card signifies major changes in the Querant's life and the complete severance from an existing set of circumstances. Such a dramatic transformation is not without pain or sense of loss but ultimately, the Querant will accept the changes as necessary and welcome the fresh start they bring in their wake. The ending of friendships, marriage or divorce, career moves, or moving house could all be signified by this card but these may not necessarily be wholly negative developments for the Querant.

> **KEY THEMES**
> dramatic change • new beginnings

Ill-dignified

Major lifestyle changes are also indicated by Death reversed although now these may be being resisted by the Querant and made more difficult as a result. The Querant may be denying the true state of a situation, and be reluctant to abandon the status quo even if he has have been stagnating in it.

> **KEY THEMES**
> resistance to change • stagnation

TEMPERANCE

Attributions

Card Number   14
Astrological Ruler   Sagittarius ♐
Key Number   25
Numerical Value   12
Hebrew Letter   Samech ס

◆ INTERPRETATIONS ◆

Dignified

In an upright orientation, Temperance signifies a period of confidence and optimism for the Querant, with the result that any problems arising during this period will be handled well. It urges the Querant to assess carefully her circumstances and to strike a balance between opposing forces within herself to give peace of mind and release inner tensions. Moderation and self-control in all aspects of the Querant's physical life are also highlighted.

KEY THEMES
self-assurance • capability • harmony

Ill-dignified

The reversed indications of Temperance are self-indulgence and disunity. The Querant may be uncertain about her direction in life and consequently may be prone to impatience, indecision and hasty judgements at this time. Conflicts of business or personal interests, or difficulties in forming partnerships are also indicated.

KEY THEMES
discord • impatience

THE DEVIL

Attributions

Card Number	15
Astrological Ruler	Capricorn ♑
Key Number	26
Numerical Value	12
Hebrew Letter	Ayin ע

◆ INTERPRETATIONS ◆

Dignified

The Devil signifies entrapment for the Querant. This can take various forms: he may be bound into a situation from which there is no escape or to people or passions that cloud reason and judgement. The Querant may seek to deny this bondage and his weaknesses. Yet he may also clearly recognise them but feel powerless to break free, circumstances leading to feelings of anger and frustration. However, the surrounding cards may suggest ways to improve the Querant's situation.

KEY THEMES
bondage • self-delusion • anger

Ill-dignified

The bondage signified by the upright card is also indicated by its reversed aspects, except that now the Querant's sense of frustration with it is even more marked. However, because of this, the Querant will begin to take steps to break free and direct his energies towards more positive goals.

KEY THEMES
increased frustration • regeneration

THE TOWER

Attributions

Card Number	16
Astrological Ruler	Mars ♂
Key Number	27
Numerical Value	9
Hebrew Letter	Peh פ

◆ Interpretations ◆

Dignified

Never a welcome card in a spread, The Tower signifies disruption, trauma and conflict. The experiences it indicates for the Querant will not be pleasant and will, probably, be unforeseen: accidents, illnesses, loss of job, house or faith are all possible outcomes. Yet bad as the card may seem, a potentially mitigating interpretation of it can be made: with a determined and positive attitude, the Querant can use such traumatic changes to provide new beginnings and opportunities for self-improvement.

KEY THEMES
drastic change • unexpected events • new life

Ill-dignified

The reversed Tower also indicates unpleasant experiences for the Querant, albeit on a lesser scale and perhaps more anticipated than signified by the upright card. However, although less traumatic, the experience and its fallout may be more protracted, with no mitigating circumstances.

KEY THEMES
less dramatic misfortune • long-term difficulties

THE STAR

Attributions

Card Number	17
Astrological Ruler	Aquarius ♒
Key Number	28
Numerical Value	12
Hebrew Letter	Tzaddi צ

✦ INTERPRETATIONS ✦

Dignified

This card is very positive and signifies a period of calm and serenity for the Querant. Difficulties are resolved and the path ahead becomes much clearer. A physical and spiritual renewal are indicated and so The Star is particularly welcome in a spead following a period of illness, or one in which the Querant's true beliefs have been severely tested. Confidence, hope, inspiration and the attainment of cherished goals will all be features of the Querant's life.

> **KEY THEMES**
> serenity • renewal • hope

Ill-dignified

Reversed, The Star warns of hopes unfulfilled, due largely to the Querant's stubborn refusal to be open to the opportunites for happiness before her. This may be due to self-doubt or pessimism stemming from past experiences and a simple distrust of 'something too good to be true'. In spite of this, the positive aspects of this card will prevail.

> **KEY THEMES**
> closed attitudes • happiness delayed

THE MOON

THE MOON

Attributions

Card Number	18
Astrological Ruler	Pisces ♓
Key Number	29
Numerical Value	12
Hebrew Letter	Qoph ק

◆ INTERPRETATIONS ◆

Dignified

This card serves as a warning to the Querant that all is not what it seems. Confusions, muddles and misunderstandings abound, due either to the Querant's own self-delusion regarding the situation or from someone else's dishonesty. Such circumstances are likely to be weighing heavily on the Querant's spirit, perhaps resulting in disillusionment and depression. The Moon urges her to rely on her instincts and intuition, rather than rational assessments, when seeking possible solutions to her difficulties.

KEY THEMES

confusion • delusion • introspection

Ill-dignified

Either way up, The Moon is an unwelcome card in a spread. The reversed aspects of the card also point to a period of confusion and bewilderment although now the scale of the problems are probably less. Health concerns are also indicated, particularly of a gynaecological nature if the Querant is female.

KEY THEMES

minor confusions • health problems

THE SUN

Attributions

Card Number	19
Astrological Ruler	The Sun ☉
Key Number	30
Numerical Value	4
Hebrew Letter	Resh ר

◆ Interpretations ◆

Dignified

The Sun indicatives positive influences at work in the Querant's life: personal achievement, material success, happiness and contentment are all signified. The Querant possesses both the skills and the drive to achieve his ambitions and the upright appearance of this card indicates that he will do so and receive recognition for his accomplishments. The Sun is very welcome if the Querant is getting married, wanting to have children, or starting out on a new venture.

KEY THEMES

success • joy • achievement

Ill-dignified

The reversed Sun also indicates success for the Querant but only after overcoming obstacles en route; these may be the result of setting unrealisticaly high goals or of the Querant's over-confidence and vanity. Personal circumstances also have clouds shadowing them but the card offers the promise of happiness in the long term.

KEY THEMES

eventual fulfilment

JUDGEMENT

Attributions

Card Number	20
Astrological Ruler	Fire △
Key Number	31
Numerical Value	3
Hebrew Letter	Shin ש

✦ INTERPRETATIONS ✦

Dignified

This is another card indicating transitory phases. In this case, however, the change signified is the natural, logical conclusion to events, rather than an abrupt ending. It is possible the Querant is facing a major decision which will begin the new phase; if so then she will be able to make it with confidence that her choice will be the right one. In this position, the Querant will be able to review recent events with some satisfaction for what she has accomplished.

KEY THEMES

change • decisions • achievement

Ill-dignified

The reversed card also indicates change, but that any assessment by the Querant of her behaviour or performance will leave a sense of regret and feelings that she could have done better; however, it is possible that the outcome of events could not have been changed and that such remorse is unjustified.

KEY THEMES

self-reproach • underachievement

THE WORLD

Attributions

Card Number	21
Astrological Ruler	Saturn ♄
Key Number	32
Numerical Value	9
Hebrew Letter	Tau ת

◆ Interpretations ◆

Dignified

The World is yet another card representing change, in this case, the successful conclusion to one phase of the Querant's life or experience and the start of another. Fulfilment and material success are indicated, but so too is a greater spiritual awareness. The Querant will feel that prior restrictions and limitations on him are now removed, ushering in a new sense of freedom and peace. On another level, travel – particularly overseas – is signified by this card.

KEY THEMES

completion • satisfaction • enlightenment

Ill-dignified

The reversed aspects of The World suggest that change has been delayed and that projects or experiences, though drawing to a close, are not yet complete. This may frustrate the Querant but patience and perseverance are recommended.

KEY THEMES

delays • disappointments

THE SUIT OF WANDS

The Suit of Wands is associated with careers, business enterprises and work in general. In astrological terms, it is associated with the element of Fire and with the signs of Aries, Leo and Sagittarius. Befitting these fiery associations, the general characteristics of the suit include creativity, inspiration, ambition, great energy and enthusiasm.

Wands are traditionally represented, not as the white-tipped black rod of the modern magician but either as fiery brands or as cut branches from which new leaves are growing. This imagery harks back to the use of thin branches from sacred trees (such as the rowan or birch) as Druidical symbols of power; it also explains the suit's correspondence to Clubs in conventional playing cards.

A preponderance of Wands in a spread will thus point strongly to career or work-related matters, particularly its organisational and creative aspects. For anyone starting a new business or similar enterprise, these are extremely informative cards to draw for a spread. It is also worth studying any subsidiary Coins cards in the spread to see what light is shed on the financial side of the project. Of course, an absence of Coins does not automatically mean the venture will be a failure. It may be that the Querant will be heavily involved in charity work for which there will be little financial reward, or it may mean that any material gain will be in the longer term. However, one thing is certain with a majority of Wands: the future will be hectic and everything will be carried out with great energy and passion.

If the court cards from this suit are to be used as significators (see p.28), the physical characteristics they are usually associated with are given in the following table.

	HAIR	EYES
Page	Red or Blonde	Blue
Knight	Blonde hair	Grey or Blue
Queen	Red or Blonde	Brown or Blue
King	Red or Blonde	Hazel or Grey

SUIT MODIFIERS
Opposite to Cups   Friendly with Swords/Coins

ACE OF WANDS

Attributions

Element	Fire
Astrological Signs	Leo ♌
	Aries ♈
	Sagittarius ♐
Life Aspect	Career & Enterprise

◆ INTERPRETATIONS ◆

Dignified

The Ace of Wands signifies the start of a new enterprise. Traditionally, this will be a new job or some other business venture, but depending on the surrounding cards, could also be interpreted as the actual birth of a child. Whatever the particular focus, creativity, enthusiasm, innovation and ambition are all indicated by this upright card and show that the Querant will be able to use these skills with great force to achieve his desire.

> **KEY THEMES**
> new beginnings • creativity • inventiveness

Ill-dignified

The reversed Ace also points to new starts but ones which are dogged by problems or are not fully implemented. It is possible the timing is wrong for such enterprises or that the Querant is lacking initiative and commitment. Poor planning, over-inflated expectations, disappointment and frustration are the inevitable results.

> **KEY THEMES**
> false starts • motivational problems • frustration

Two of Wands

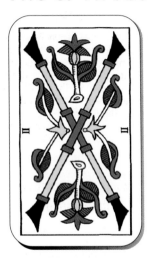

Attributions

Element	Fire
Astrological Signs	Leo ♌
	Aries ♈
	Sagittarius ♐
Life Aspect	Career & Enterprise

✦ INTERPRETATIONS ✦

Dignified

The upright Two of Wands is generally a good card to draw. It signifies the successful attainment of targets and the due rewards this brings the Querant (financial security, promotion, etc.). It also strongly suggests that these may be the result of, or lead to, some form of partnership or joint venture which will be beneficial for the Querant. Yet, running concurrently with these positive aspects, there are also indications of self-doubt and anxiety for the future.

KEY THEMES
achievement • partnership • anxiety

Ill-dignified

The reverse indicators of this card point to problems with partners, particularly in business. They also suggest that the less positive qualities associated with the upright card begin to dominate; the Querant begins to question the worth of what she has achieved and the personal values she has adopted to allow her to fulfill her ambitions.

KEY THEMES
partnership difficulties • self-doubt

THREE OF WANDS

Attributions

Element	Fire
Astrological Signs	Leo ♌
	Aries ♈
	Sagittarius ♐
Life Aspect	Career & Enterprise

◆ Interpretations ◆

Dignified

Upright, this card signifies the beginning of a very productive period, particularly if new career opportunites or new commercial ventures are being considered. Any such projects requiring creativity, inventiveness and initiative are well-starred although the rewards will come in the longer-term, rather than immediately. Success is indicated especially if the venture involves partnership, particularly one offering practical assistance and knowledge.

KEY THEMES
new starts • long-term success • partnership

Ill-dignified

Reversed, this card signifies false starts, missed opportunities and squandered talents. New ventures are destined to run into difficulties, in spite perhaps of early successes. The problems may lie in personality clashes, in the Querant's unrealistic ambitions, in an obstinate refusal of help, or a misdirection of effort.

KEY THEMES
commercial problems • misdirected efforts

FOUR OF WANDS

Attributions

Element	Fire
Astrological Signs	Leo ♌
	Aries ♈
	Sagittarius ♐
Life Aspect	Career & Enterprise

◆ Interpretations ◆

Dignified

The upright aspects of this card point to the successful completion of a project or of some relationship which brings in its wake a profound sense of peace, security and harmony. Endings however are often the prelude to beginnings and this card signifies in particular fresh starts in relation to the home. Thus, house-buying or -moving is favourably indicated. Also, depending on the surrounding cards, a new romance or even a wedding is indicated, either possibly involving a house-move.

KEY THEMES
successful completion • fresh starts • house-moves

Ill-dignified

Even when reversed, this is not a bad card. The happy conclusion indicated by the upright card may now be delayed and although further effort may be required to secure this state, some comfort can be derived from the fact that the end is in sight and that current difficulties are only likely to be temporary.

KEY THEMES
temporary delays • renewed effort required

FIVE OF WANDS

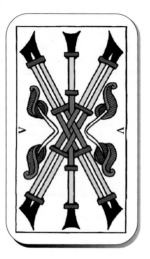

Attributions

Element	Fire
Astrological Signs	Leo ♌
	Aries ♈
	Sagittarius ♐
Life Aspect	Career & Enterprise

◆ INTERPRETATIONS ◆

Dignified

The traditional interpretation of the Five of Wands is of struggle and aggravation. The surrounding cards will indicate the main area of the Querant's life in which these difficulties will be experienced. Whatever this is, the root causes will be the same: competitiveness and opposition to forces that limit the Querant's freedom. Frustration and anxiety may be common feelings but hard work and perseverance will allow the Querant to overcome the obstacles before him.

> **KEY THEMES**
> strife • competitiveness • anxiety

Ill-dignified

In a reversed orientation, the Five of Wands points to more serious difficulties for the Querant. The competitiveness indicated in the upright card may now be particularly bitter and at times may result in spiteful and underhand behaviour. The reversed Five also warns of possible legal entanglements.

> **KEY THEMES**
> serious problems • legal difficulties • acrimony

SIX OF WANDS

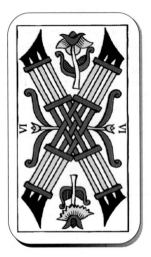

Attributions

Element	Fire
Astrological Signs	Leo ♌
	Aries ♈
	Sagittarius ♐
Life Aspect	Career & Enterprise

◆ INTERPRETATIONS ◆

Dignified

The upright Six of Wands is the card of triumph and success. It indicates that the Querant's past efforts in a given field will bear fruit and she will now be able to enjoy the rewards and recognition that this brings. With such success, however, comes the advice that the Querant should be magnanimous in victory and seek reconciliation with those less fortunate rivals. If the Querant is awaiting the outcome of some event or project, then this card indicates that the news will be favourable.

KEY THEMES

triumph • recognition • good news

Ill-dignified

When reversed, this card indicates that problems will dog the Querant and that long-awaited news of the outcome of an event or project will be delayed further or will not be good. Misunderstandings with colleagues and problems with communications, personal and mechanical, are also signified.

KEY THEMES

continuing problems • delayed or bad news

SEVEN OF WANDS

Attributions

Element	Fire
Astrological Signs	Leo ♌
	Aries ♈
	Sagittarius ♐
Life Aspect	Career & Enterprise

◆ INTERPRETATIONS ◆

Dignified

This card warns of major conflicts and challenges confronting the Querant. These may be as straight-forward as an exam but it could also signify a more serious personal struggle at work or in relationships. However, the upright Seven also indicates the Querant's great reserves of courage, integrity and stamina. The resolution may seem some way off but if the Querant maintains his position and faces up to the challenge, the prospects for success are good.

KEY THEMES
testing times • courage • longer term successes

Ill-dignified

The reversed Seven indicates that when facing such trials and tests, or his position is challenged, the Querant's courage is likely to fail him and he will back away from the confrontation. This will be unfortunate because his position is probably stronger than he imagines and this loss of confidence will result in important opportunites being lost.

KEY THEMES
lack of courage • lost opportunities

EIGHT OF WANDS

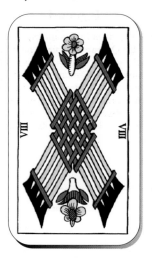

Attributions

Element	Fire
Astrological Signs	Leo ♌
	Aries ♈
	Sagittarius ♐
Life Aspect	Career & Enterprise

◆ Interpretations ◆

Dignified

The Eight of Wands points to the marked increase in the tempo of the Querant's affairs. Projects begun will progress swiftly and without delay, while those already in motion will be brought to a speedy and generally satisfactory conclusion. The prospect of travel, associated particularly with business affairs, is also indicated. Romance is also well-starred under this card, particularly if major decisions are in the process of being made.

KEY THEMES
speedy actions • end to delay • travel

Ill-dignified

In its reversed aspects, this card warns against the dangers of advancing too quickly: the swift progress and other positive features of the upright card could be negated by overeagerness leading to rash or ill-considered judgements, and wasted effort. Delays feature strongly and the Querant's plans may have to be postponed.

KEY THEMES
overeagerness • poor judgement • delays

NINE OF WANDS

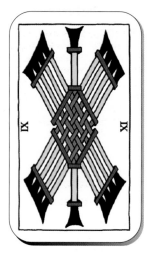

Attributions

Element	Fire
Astrological Signs	Leo ♌
	Aries ♈
	Sagittarius ♐
Life Aspect	Career & Enterprise

✦ INTERPRETATIONS ✦

Dignified

The Nine of Wands signifies that the Querant has a strong and resourceful character and that she will have to draw heavily upon it to see her through forthcoming difficulties. Life may presently be comfortable but a number of personal and/or professional problems are approaching. The Querant should maintain her status quo and then use the strong foundations she has already established in these areas to move forward when opportunities to progress arise.

KEY THEMES
inner strengths • temporary security

Ill-dignified

Reversed, the Nine indicates a lack of initiative and flexibility on the part of the Querant. Coupled to an obstinate streak, these traits lead the Querant to pursue failed ventures or strategies which will patently fail to bring about her desired goals. New approaches and an ability to adapt in a changing environment are essential.

KEY THEMES
inflexibility • poor initiative

TEN OF WANDS

Attributions

Element	Fire
Astrological Signs	Leo ♌
	Aries ♈
	Sagittarius ♐
Life Aspect	Career & Enterprise

✦ INTERPRETATIONS ✦

Dignified

This card signifies the burdens of excessive work for the Querant. It may simply mean that he is taking on too much in pursuit of his goals; on the other hand, it may be that this excessive workload is the result of having already achieved them, e.g. new responsibilities following a promotion or having expanded a business beyond a certain level. This burden may become oppressive as the Querant juggles with conflicting business and social demands.

KEY THEMES

overcommitment • oppression

Ill-dignified

Reversed, this card indicates that the Querant is buckling under the strain of this excessive workload and that much of the pressure is self-inflicted: a mistrust of colleagues and a reluctance to delegate tasks or responsibilities is likely to underpin most of the Querant's problems. Also indicated is the Querant's misuse of position or power to oppress others.

KEY THEMES

excessive burdens • mistrust • abuse of power

PAGE OF WANDS

PAGE OF WANDS

Attributions

Element	Fire
Astrological Signs	Leo ♌
	Aries ♈
	Sagittarius ♐
Life Aspect	Career & Enterprise

✦ Interpretations ✦

Dignified

The personal characteristics indicated by the upright Page are great energy, intelligence, resourcefulness and loyalty, and are usually associated with a young male. With regard to situations, this card points to good news coming to the Querant (either from or about a youngster), which may be unexpected. It also signifies a new beginning and can point to the Querant starting a new project with great energy and creativity.

> **KEY THEMES**
> energy • loyalty • new beginnings

Ill-dignified

The reversed personality traits of this card include a domineering attitude, shallowness and over-ambition, characteristics which could pose problems for any young man who is signified in the spread. The reversed Page also indicates either the arrival of bad news for the Querant or the late arrival of better tidings.

> **KEY THEMES**
> domineering attitude • bad news

KNIGHT OF WANDS

KNIGHT OF WANDS

Attributions

Element	Fire
Astrological Signs	Leo ♌
	Aries ♈
	Sagittarius ♐
Life Aspect	Career & Enterprise

◆ Interpretations ◆

Dignified

Changeability is the key interpretation of this card. It represents someone who thrives on being unpredictable, someone who can alter his position, viewpoint or direction quickly and without warning, leaving others in his wake. However, his eloquence, charm and sophistication usually ensure his popularity in spite of this. If referring to a situation, this card usually indicates a changing environment for the Querant, either through travel, perhaps undertaken at short notice, or a change of residence.

KEY THEMES

changeability • unpredictability • foreign travel

Ill-dignified

Reversed, this card signifies a young man who is intolerant and boastful, someone who is generally associated with disharmony and friction. Other interpretations signify difficulties concerning personal relationships, journeys or property transactions, possibly arising from the Querant's indecisiveness.

KEY THEMES

contentiousness • travel problems • indecisiveness

QUEEN OF WANDS

QUEEN OF WANDS

Attributions

Element	Fire
Astrological Signs	Leo ♌
	Aries ♈
	Sagittarius ♐
Life Aspect	Career & Enterprise

◆ INTERPRETATIONS ◆

Dignified

Upright, the Queen of Wands usually indicates a mature woman who is practical, generous and gregarious, someone with a strongly independent streak to their nature who, at the same time, is capable of showing great attachment to home and family. This card can represent the Querant herself but depending on the spread may indicate someone on whom she can depend or turn to for advice or help.

KEY THEMES

gregarious woman • independent yet home-loving

Ill-dignified

Reversed, the fiery nature of the suit comes to the fore and the ill-dignified Queen signifies a petty, cruel and domineering woman, someone with an overinflated view of her talents who imposes herself where she can do little good. As someone who takes offence easily and bears great grudges, she is a bad enemy. The card also points to possible infidelities in relationships.

KEY THEMES

domineering personality • unfaithfulness

KING OF WANDS

KING OF WANDS

Attributions

Element	Fire
Astrological Signs	Leo ♌
	Aries ♈
	Sagittarius ♐
Life Aspect	Career & Enterprise

◆ INTERPRETATIONS ◆

Dignified

As a personality, the upright King of Wands signifies a mature man of position or authority – energetic, enterprising and possessing great integrity. He is an effective leader and a skilled arbitrator and it is in this latter capacity that he may be involved in the Querant's life, acting to resolve a dispute. The card also indicates the possibility of an unexpected financial windfall, perhaps from an inheritance.

KEY THEMES
authority figure • mediation • monetary gain

Ill-dignified

Ill-dignified, the King's personality traits include intolerance, over-bearing strictness and unreliability. He will try to impose his views and values on others, believing them to be superior, and will show little respect for a different viewpoint. The card may also point to an upcoming dispute and serves as a warning to the Querant to extract themselves from it at the earliest opportunity.

KEY THEMES
domineering personality • intolerance • disputes

THE SUIT OF CUPS

The suit of Cups is identified primarily with the emotional aspects of our everyday lives, although the creative arts are also associated with this suit. Astrologically, it is associated with the element of Water and the three Water signs: Pisces, Cancer and Scorpio. General characteristics of this suit include increased sensitivity, self-awareness and vulnerability.

Although corresponding to Hearts in conventional playing cards, Cups in a tarot spread should not be interpreted only with regard to the Querant's love life: love is only one of a range of emotions that we feel – hate, joy, sadness, fear and lust also feature in people's experiences and all these can be reflected in this suit of deep feelings.

Where a majority of Cups appears in a spread, it will be clear then that it relates to the Querant's emotional life. As such, it should strike a note of caution in the Reader. Because the suit relates to feelings, rather than facts, it can be difficult to interpret correctly because what the Querant feels about something or somebody may not always accurately reflect the reality of a situation which could have a very different bearing on your reading of a scenario. To assist you when faced with a majority of Cups, it is always a good policy to examine the subsidiary majority (i.e. the next most numerous suit) to see if a factual base to the reading can be established.

As already discussed (see p.28), while in some spreads court cards can be identified with individuals, at other times they will instead represent specific situations involving the Querant. It can be difficult to identify which is which and it may be wise to consider interpretations for each in order to judge what is most appropriate in the context of the surrounding cards. Traditionally, knights and pages most often represent situations in a spread. If Cup court cards are used as significators, the physical characteristics they are usually associated with are given in the following table.

	HAIR	EYES
Page	Brown	Blue or Brown
Knight	Brown	Grey or Blue
Queen	Golden Brown	Blue
King	Fair	Blue

SUIT MODIFIERS	
Opposite to Wands	Friendly with Swords/Coins

ACE OF CUPS

Attributions

Element	Water
Astrological Signs	Pisces ♓
	Cancer ♋
	Scorpio ♏
Life Aspect	Emotions

✦ INTERPRETATIONS ✦

Dignified

Aces generally signify new beginnings and the Ace of Cups indicates the start of a very auspicious period for the Querant: joy, happiness, and love will all feature in good measure in his life. Personal relationships, whether close companionship, romance or even marriage, are particularly favoured. Also, since the ruling element, Water, is associated with the feminine aspects of nature, which stress sensitivity, self-awareness and intuition, creative out-pourings or spiritual experiences are also indicated.

KEY THEMES
happiness • deep relationships • creativity

Ill-dignified

The reversed Ace points to emotional upheaval in the Querant's life. This is likely to leave him feeling insecure, dissatisfied and possibly unwanted. Such feelings may arise from a currently unhappy relationship or follow in the wake of a break-up.

KEY THEMES
emotional upsets • insecurity • anxiety

Two of Cups

Attributions

Element	Water
Astrological Signs	Pisces ♓
	Cancer ♋
	Scorpio ♏
Life Aspect	Emotions

✦ INTERPRETATIONS ✦

Dignified

The key interpretation of the Two of Cups is that of partnership: it indicates that the Querant has, or is about to enter, a powerful relationship with someone for whom they have a great regard and trust. This can, of course, be a love affair and the appearance of this card in a spread points to lasting happiness. It may, however, refer to a business relationship and in this case would indicate a greater understanding and co-operation between partners. In this context it can also point to a resolution of professional differences.

KEY THEMES
relationships • love • affinity

Ill-dignified

The negative aspects of this card indicate quarrels and misunderstandings with partners, possibly leading to the ending of a relationship, be it personal or professional. The Querant must guard against rash actions and hasty decisions lest they precipitate a course of events that is subsequently regretted.

KEY THEMES
troubled relationships • precipitous actions

THREE OF CUPS

Attributions

Element	Water
Astrological Signs	Pisces ♓
	Cancer ♋
	Scorpio ♏
Life Aspect	Emotions

✦ INTERPRETATIONS ✦

Dignified

The upright Three points to great happiness and an abundance of good fortune in the Querant's life. She will be feeling secure, prosperous and fulfilled and will wish to share these feelings with those close to her. Specifically, a celebration for the Querant is in the offing, perhaps arising from the successful completion of an important project, or indeed from the birth of a child. The card can also indicate the start of an important creative period for the Querant.

KEY THEMES

abundance • celebration • creativity

Ill-dignified

The abundance of the upright card has turned to over-indulgence when reversed, leading to selfishness and the exploitation of others. Also, a meanness of spirit and intolerant attitude is casting a shadow on a potentially rewarding relationship for the Querant. Marital problems in particular are highlighted by this card.

KEY THEMES

selfishness • relationship problems

FOUR OF CUPS

Attributions

Element	Water
Astrological Signs	Pisces ♓
	Cancer ♋
	Scorpio ♏
Life Aspect	Emotions

✦ Interpretations ✦

Dignified

As with the previous card, the Four of Cups points to much that is good in the Querant's life. Now, however, instead of this producing positive feelings, it generates a sense of apathy and boredom. Although secure, the sense of excitement is missing from his life which has become boring and all too familiar. Thus, a re-evaluation of his life and aims is needed to provide new directions, new stimulations and new challenges.

KEY THEMES
boredom • dissatisfaction • re-evaluation

Ill-dignified

Reversed, this card indicates that the Querant's boredom with his lifestyle is in danger of degenerating into self-pity and lethargy, making it increasingly difficult for him to motivate himself to make the changes that are necessary. Depression may also be at the root of health problems.

KEY THEMES
apathy • depression • lethargy

FIVE OF CUPS

Attributions

Element	Water
Astrological Signs	Pisces ♓
	Cancer ♋
	Scorpio ♏
Life Aspect	Emotions

◆ INTERPRETATIONS ◆

Dignified

Fives are traditionally unwelcome cards to draw and, when coupled to the emotions of the suit of Cups, indicates very negative influences in the Querant's life. This is a card of loss and disappointment, particularly with regard to to personal relationships. The loss need not be current; it may have happened some time ago but the heartache caused by it is still fresh. Yet with a positive attitude, the Querant may overcome her regret and find hope and new direction in her current situation.

KEY THEMES

loss • regret • new hope

Ill-dignified

Reversed, the Five points to better times ahead. The regret associated with the upright card remains but is diminishing with the passage of time and the Querant will be able to start building for a new future. New starts often bring new uncertainties but her past experiences will provide valuable lessons.

KEY THEMES

a hopeful future • learning from the past

SIX OF CUPS

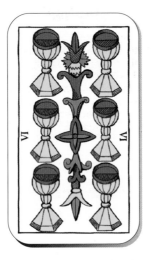

Attributions

Element   Water
Astrological Signs   Pisces ♓
Cancer ♋
Scorpio ♏
Life Aspect   Emotions

✦ INTERPRETATIONS ✦

Dignified

A generally positive card, the Six signifies great harmony in the Querant's life, a condition which has its roots firmly in his past, possibly even as far back as childhood. Past associations or efforts are now bearing fruit for the Querant who is basking in the pleasure this brings. Happy reminiscences, old friends or even past lovers are all likely to feature currently in his life. Another element of this card is the indication of a new job or residence.

KEY THEMES
reminiscences • past associations

Ill-dignified

The reversed Six signifies the Querant's tendency to live too much in the past. He is seeking to escape from current problems by taking refuge in memories of happier times, but such wallowing in nostalgia is preventing him from taking the steps necessary to address and resolve these present difficulties.

KEY THEMES
living in the past • self-delusion

SEVEN OF CUPS

Attributions

Element	Water
Astrological Signs	Pisces ♓
	Cancer ♋
	Scorpio ♏
Life Aspect	Emotions

✦ INTERPRETATIONS ✦

Dignified

The emotions chiefly associated with this card are those stemming from within, from the imagination and the unconscious mind, and they represent the Querant's hopes, desires and aspirations. Unfortunately, the card also indicates an element of confusion as to which of these represent an achievable reality and which are simply pipe-dreams. It is important that the Querant chooses wisely which paths to follow, but it may be that now is not the time to decide.

KEY THEMES
dreams and aspirations • confusion

Ill-dignified

Reversal indicates that the Querant is tending towards self-delusion and an unrealistic assessment of their present circumstances. The effects of this on her life-choices could be serious and the surrounding cards may shed some light on this. It is time for the Querant to ground herself in reality.

KEY THEMES
self-delusion • wrong choices

EIGHT OF CUPS

Attributions

Element	Water
Astrological Signs	Pisces ♓
	Cancer ♋
	Scorpio ♏
Life Aspect	Emotions

◆ INTERPRETATIONS ◆

Dignified

The upright Eight of Cups suggests that, in spite of stability and security, the Querant is likely to be dissatisfied with his current life and is drawn towards new pastures and challenges. Underpinning this is a yearning for a greater understanding of his inner self and the need to find a deeper meaning to his life. This may lead to a rejection of existing, unfulfilling, relationships, ways of thinking and lifestyles and the start of a period of new personal growth.

KEY THEMES
lifestyle changes • personal development

Ill-dignified

The Querant's restlessness is also a feature of the reversed card, except now there is a danger of him recklessly pursuing a very uncertain future, abandoning those things of value in his life for what may in fact be little more than a fantasy. The card serves as warning against making major lifestyle changes at this time.

KEY THEMES
recklessness • unrealistic expectations

NINE OF CUPS

Attributions

Element	Water
Astrological Signs	Pisces ♓
	Cancer ♋
	Scorpio ♏
Life Aspect	Emotions

◆ INTERPRETATIONS ◆

Dignified

In an upright orientation, this is a very positive card. A period of well-being, contentment and great happiness is indicated for the Querant, one in which a range of personal wishes will be realised. Creativity is also favoured at this time and past efforts will now reap rewards as projects move towards a satisfactory conclusion. The Querant has much to enjoy and wishes to share this with others less fortuante.

KEY THEMES
happiness • contentment • generosity

Ill-dignified

This card now points to complacency and self-satisfaction. Although superficially happy and secure, all may not be as it seems and the Querant may be ignoring an underlying problem, something she may later regret. The reversed Nine also indicates that the Querant has a vain and self-congratulatory regard for her present good fortune which devalues what she has achieved in others' eyes.

KEY THEMES
complacency • superficiality • lack of humility

TEN OF CUPS

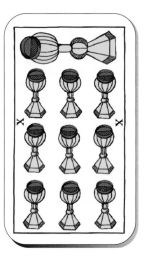

Attributions

Element	Water
Astrological Signs	Pisces ♓
	Cancer ♋
	Scorpio ♏
Life Aspect	Emotions

◆ Interpretations ◆

Dignified

This card signifies the final attainment of some long-sought-after goal which brings in its wake great happiness and fulfilment for the Querant. Emotional commitments, both individually and collectively, are also strongly signified by the upright Ten. Doubts about holding particular viewpoints or supporting causes are resolved, family tensions and frictions are healed, and for newly weds or those considering marriage, this is a most auspicious card to draw as it traditionally represents long and happy unions.

KEY THEMES

achievement • commitment • good marriage

Ill-dignified

The reversed aspects of this card indicate tension and disruption to a previously happy environment. The Querant's relationships are likely to be rather stormy, both within his wider family and also with friends and partners. He may be feeling depressed and let-down by those around him, perhaps justifiably.

KEY THEMES

tense relationships • disruption • unhappiness

PAGE OF CUPS

PAGE OF CUPS

Attributions

Element	Water
Astrological Signs	Pisces ♓
	Cancer ♋
	Scorpio ♏
Life Aspect	Emotions

◆ Interpretations ◆

Dignified

When representing an individual, the Page of Cups indicates a quiet, introspective, gentle youngster, artistically gifted but who tends not to advertise his or her talents. This is a person who will be in a position to assist the Querant to a specified goal. As a situation, and depending on the surrounding spread, good news will be forthcoming, for example, of a birth, or of an engagement or marriage. New creative projects and periods of study are also indicated.

KEY THEMES
good news • creative outlets

Ill-dignified

Reversed, this card indicates a youngster who, though talented, squanders his or her energies on frivolous flights of fancy. This person can be lethargic to the point of idleness and often displays a lack of commitment and staying power. Situationally, the Querant may be the victim of a deception which comes to light.

KEY THEMES
wasted talents • idleness • poor commitment

KNIGHT OF CUPS

KNIGHT OF CUPS

Attributions

Element	Water
Astrological Signs	Pisces ♓
	Cancer ♋
	Scorpio ♏
Life Aspect	Emotions

◆ INTERPRETATIONS ◆

Dignified

The Knight of Cups is a sensitive, idealistic and romantic young man. He has great originality and inventiveness but a passive nature leads him to be distracted from his goals by those around him or by capricious flights of fancy. Alternative interpretations of this card point to new initiatives involving the Querant, possibly regarding his personal relationships and in some way connected to the person represented by the card, or perhaps concerning some artistic or otherwise creative pursuit.

KEY THEMES

easily led • new opportunities • creativity

Ill-dignified

Deception is a major aspect of this reversed card. In terms of personality, the reversed Knight may not be all that he seems and superficial pleasantness may be shielding a darker character. Similarly, the Querant should take great care in his personal and business affairs as problems may be lurking unseen, perhaps because of someone's treachery.

KEY THEMES

deception • underhand behaviour

QUEEN OF CUPS

QUEEN OF CUPS

Attributions

Element	Water
Astrological Signs	Pisces ♓
	Cancer ♋
	Scorpio ♏
Life Aspect	Emotions

◆ INTERPRETATIONS ◆

Dignified

The Queen of Cups signifies a sensitive, affectionate and receptive woman. As with personalities associated with the other court cards of this suit, her character is essentially passive but she is in close touch with her inner self and can demonstrate great perceptiveness, intuition and will-power when needed. For men who draw this card, it may serve as a gentle reminder not to suppress the feminine aspects of their personality and to open themselves to the whole spectrum of life's emotions.

KEY THEMES
sensitive, mature woman • intuition

Ill-dignified

Superfically, the woman represented by the reversed Queen may appear to have many of the qualities of her upright sister. However, she is in fact more likely to be fickle, vain, untrustworthy and capricious. As such she can be the source of great problems to anyone who allows her into their confidence.

KEY THEMES
unreliable woman • unstable character

KING OF CUPS

KING OF CUPS

Attributions

Element	Water
Astrological Signs	Pisces ♓
	Cancer ♋
	Scorpio ♏
Life Aspect	Emotions

◆ Interpretations ◆

Dignified

This card represents an intelligent, respected, mature man, most likely a professional or businessman in a position of authority. His calm, amiable personality often hides the intensity of his feelings which are kept under tight rein; as a result, he can appear unconcerned and distant. However, this person is likely to advise the Querant well (perhaps on a professional basis) on a matter of great importance.

KEY THEMES

authoritative, mature man • sound advice

Ill-dignified

As with other court cards in this suit, deception and underhand behaviour are signified by this card reversed. Now this character combines intelligence and authority with dishonesty and unscrupulousness and represents someone who could be a major threat to the Querant; the surrounding cards may indicate a particular area for her to watch in this respect. In general, this is a person to be avoided.

KEY THEMES

deception • dishonesty • threat

THE SUIT OF SWORDS

The Suit of Swords represents our intellectual and rational faculties, in other words the mental aspects of our lives. Positive characteristics associated with these cards include strength, authority, courage and ambition. However, because it is associated with the masculine astrological element of Air, the suit is also said to represent conflict and animosity, producing the negative characteristics of pain, anger and aggression. Above all, Swords indicate a desire to seek the truth and it is this desire to call 'a spade a spade' (which incidentally is the suit's equivalent in a convential card deck) that perhaps give rise to the conflict associated with this suit: the truth of a matter is not always to everyone's liking and its relentless pursuit can give rise to animosity and resentment.

Not surprisingly then, a predominance of Swords in a spread can at first seem to be an indicator of bad tidings – traditionally they are said to portend arguments, illnesses, and even death. Yet because they represent intangible elements of the human mind rather than hard facts, Sword majorities need to be interpreted with some care. As lifestyles grow ever more complex and stressful, this will naturally be reflected in tarot spreads; remember, however, that the Querant's worries and concerns about a situation may not always accurately reflect the reality of it which could have a very different bearing on your reading of a scenario. Subsidiary majorities in the spread should provide an indication of general areas of concern for the Querant (Cups for domestic or relationship difficulties, Coins for financial problems and Wands for difficulties at work) as well as pointers to the outcome which should be interpreted in the light of the Querant's views on the area under scrutiny.

The Sword court cards represent people born under the Air signs, i.e. Gemini, Libra and Aquarius. If you wish to use these cards as Significators, then the complexions usually associated with them are listed in the table below.

	HAIR	EYES
Page	Light Brown	Blue
Knight	Dark Brown	Dark
Queen	Light Brown	Grey
King	Black	Dark

SUIT MODIFIERS
Opposite to Coins   Friendly with Cups/Wands

ACE OF SWORDS

Attributions

Element	Air
Astrological Signs	Gemini ♊
	Libra ♎
	Aquarius ♒
Life Experience	Intellectual activity

◆ INTERPRETATIONS ◆

Dignified

Tarot aces are traditionally seen as the absolute embodiment of the astrological element associated with each suit. For Swords, the upright Ace indicates a high degree of mental clarity and intellectual focus. In practical terms, this usually means that the Querant, largely by strength of will, has decisively overcome obstacles in his path and will be embarking on a new period of his life which will eventually bring much reward.

KEY THEMES
mental focus • new beginnings • success

Ill-dignified

The reversed Ace indicates that the Querant may be being overly rational in his affairs and is riding roughshod over the feelings of others in pursuit of his goals. It can also point to a situation in which the Querant is misusing his intellectual superiority, resorting to underhand, dishonest dealings. Legal problems or with authority in general are indicated.

KEY THEMES
abuse of power • injustice

TWO OF SWORDS

Attributions

Element	Air
Astrological Signs	Gemini ♊
	Libra ♎
	Aquarius ♒
Life Experience	Intellectual activity

✦ Interpretations ✦

Dignified

Ironically for a suit that is strongly associated with discord, its upright Two is seen to represent harmony and healing, the balancing of two opposing forces or issues. The source of conflict may be external in which the Querant is acting as mediator or is trying to initiate an honourable settlement; on the other hand, it may be an inner struggle as the Querant's heart and mind pull in different directions. Whatever the cause of the discord, its resolution brings with it a true sense of peace and relief for the Querant.

KEY THEMES

balance • peace of mind • resolution of conflict

Ill-dignified

The reversed aspects of this card revert to the true nature of the suit. Differences between opposing viewpoints prove irreconcilable; whatever balance or restraint existing between them breaks down and conflict ensues.

KEY THEMES

irreconcilable differences • disharmony

THREE OF SWORDS

Attributions

Element	Air
Astrological Signs	Gemini ♊
	Libra ♎
	Aquarius ♒
Life Experience	Intellectual activity

◆ INTERPRETATIONS ◆

Dignified

An unhappy card, the appearance of the Three of Swords points to a deep heartache felt by the Querant. There is much pain and conflict in her life, which has either caused, or is the result of, the ending of a partnership, professional or personal. As with Death in the Major Arcana, this ending may signify a new beginning for the Querant – particularly if she chooses to address her problems honestly – but the transition will undoubtedly bring with it hurt and a sense of alienation.

KEY THEMES

separation • unhappiness • fresh starts

Ill-dignified

When the card is reversed, the negative traits of the upright Three are exacerbated. So the Querant's hurt is likely to be more deeply felt, the separation more painful and acrimonious, and the entire sorry situation will be drawn out over a more extended period.

KEY THEMES

pain • acrimony • prolonged heartache

Four of Swords

Attributions

Element	Air
Astrological Signs	Gemini ♊
	Libra ♎
	Aquarius ♒
Life Experience	Intellectual activity

◆ INTERPRETATIONS ◆

Dignified

The fours traditionally represent order and stability and, when applied to the inherent qualities of Swords, this card indicates that the Querant will soon enjoy a respite from his problems – if only temporarily. Nevertheless, the Querant will have an opportunity to rest and recover, perhaps having retreated to a place of seclusion to free himself from the stresses and tensions that have been weighing him down. Recovery from an illness can be a specific interpretation of the Four of Swords.

KEY THEMES
rest • withdrawal • healing

Ill-dignified

The reversed aspects of this card suggest that the Querant has withdrawn too far into himself and this isolation may be becoming a negative influence: instead of renewing his mental and physical energies, he is feeling cut off or rejected. It is possible that this isolation has been forced on the Querant who, naturally, resents it.

KEY THEMES
isolation • rejection • exclusion

FIVE OF SWORDS

Attributions

Element	Air
Astrological Signs	Gemini ♊
	Libra ♎
	Aquarius ♒
Life Experience	Intellectual activity

✦ INTERPRETATIONS ✦

Dignified

This is a card of conflict and defeat. Having been engaged in a dispute with someone, the Querant is likely to have lost heavily and has been forced to retire to lick her wounds. Consequently, her pride and self-esteem may be at a low ebb and there is the danger of becoming trapped in a cycle of negative thoughts and attitudes. However, if she can accept the defeat gracefully, she will be able to overcome any lingering sense of humiliation and move on to new challenges.

KEY THEMES
defeat • low self-esteem

Ill-dignified

The ill-dignified Five of Swords generally indicates malicious, divisive or unethical behaviour, either directed at the Querant or perpetrated by her. If the victim, then her sense of defeat will be great; if she is the instigator of this intrigue, then any victory arising from it is likely to be a Pyrrhic one.

KEY THEMES
deception • malice

SIX OF SWORDS

Attributions

Element	Air
Astrological Signs	Gemini ♊
	Libra ♎
	Aquarius ♒
Life Experience	Intellectual activity

✦ INTERPRETATIONS ✦

Dignified

The Six represents the prospect of better times ahead for the Querant. He will be able to put current problems and difficulties behind him, largely as the result of applying himself mentally rather than physically. But typically of Swords, any positive aspects to the card are usually qualified; in this case, trouble still lies ahead for the Querant and the passage to his new life will not be easy. However, the worst is over and peace of mind will be achieved. A long journey, perhaps over water, is also indicated.

KEY THEMES

better future • residual difficulties • a journey

Ill-dignified

With a reversed orientation, this card indicates that the Querant is refusing to face fully the problems confronting him. Temporary, half-hearted solutions will bring only temporary relief and the source of difficulty remains. The Querant must address and resolve the root problem before he can move on.

KEY THEMES

procrastination • limited relief

SEVEN OF SWORDS

Attributions

Element	Air
Astrological Signs	Gemini ♊
	Libra ♎
	Aquarius ♒
Life Experience	Intellectual activity

◆ INTERPRETATIONS ◆

Dignified

The Seven indicates that the Querant is facing sustained opposition from a particular source, although it may not yet be clear who is the driving force behind this. Plans are upset and progress hindered, which may leave the Querant feeling frustrated and with a sense that continuing will be futile. However, by avoiding direct confrontation, by careful and diligent preparation, and by the intelligent and skilful use of her talents, she may yet be able to overcome this unknown but more powerful opponent.

KEY THEMES
unknown opponents • avoiding confrontation

Ill-dignified

The reversed Seven serves as a warning to the Querant not to relax her vigilance or efforts if only partial successes are gained over an opponent. Similarly, any weaknesses in her personality such as timidity or indecisiveness may allow her opponents to recover ground to her detriment.

KEY THEMES
vigilance • sustained effort • character flaws

Eight of Swords

Attributions

Element	Air
Astrological Signs	Gemini ♊
	Libra ♎
	Aquarius ♒
Life Experience	Intellectual activity

◆ INTERPRETATIONS ◆

Dignified

Blocked energy is the principle indicator of this card. The Querant is likely to find himself in a situation where he would like to follow through a range of exciting opportunities and ideas but forces beyond his control are restricting his options and movements. The resultant frustration may in turn lead to anxiety or a loss of faith in what he is trying to achieve but the Querant's best course is to accept the delays patiently and wait for the situation to change.

KEY THEMES

frustration • restriction • disillusionment

Ill-dignified

With the reversed card, the Querant's feelings of being trapped are more intense and his pessimism is heightened by a growing sense of isolation, perhaps following an estrangement from family or friends as a result of a quarrel. It is imperative that the Querant breaks free of this negative cycle and confronts the problems besetting him.

KEY THEMES

isolation • feeling trapped

NINE OF SWORDS

Attributions

Element   Air
Astrological Signs   Gemini ♊
     Libra ♎
     Aquarius ♒
Life Experience   Intellectual activity

✦ INTERPRETATIONS ✦

Dignified

The Nine of Swords represents the extreme of mental pain and anguish felt by the Querant. She will be too ready to put herself down and she fears what others think of her or say about her behind her back. Such worries – perhaps unfounded but real nevertheless – create great anxiety, depression and nervous tension. Traditionally, this card is associated with accidents and illnesses and also with violence and cruelty. Spreads involving this card therefore must be interpreted with great care and the surrounding cards may provide vital clues to assist an accurate reading.

KEY THEMES

mental anguish • self-deprecation • accidents

Ill-dignified

The reversed indications of the Nine are very black indeed. The Querant is likely to be trapped in a vicious cycle of despair and despondency which often exacerbate the problems behind them, and so perptuate them. Paralysed by self-doubt, she will be unable to break out of this negative cycle without outside help.

KEY THEMES

deep despair • self-doubt

TEN OF SWORDS

Attributions

Element	Air
Astrological Signs	Gemini ♊
	Libra ♎
	Aquarius ♒
Life Experience	Intellectual activity

◆ Interpretations ◆

Dignified

This is traditionally the most feared card in the deck. It represents unavoidable disaster and ruination for the Querant, a situation which will bring much anguish and desolation. In practical terms, it may represent a complete failure of plans or of an enterprise, perhaps as a result of the treacherous acts of enemies. The only consolation to be taken from this is that the resolution of the problem is at hand and from the ruins, the Querant will be able to start afresh.

KEY THEMES
ruin • failure • new hope

Ill-dignified

Reversed, the Ten indicates that, if anything, the difficult situation facing the Querant is going to get much worse. Traditionally, this card is said to represent a death, depending on the surrounding cards, but this should never be intimated to the Querant for fear of unjustly causing alarm.

KEY THEMES
worsening conditions • major problems

PAGE OF SWORDS

PAGE OF SWORDS

Attributions

Element	Air
Astrological Signs	Gemini ♊
	Libra ♎
	Aquarius ♒
Life Experience	Intellectual activity

◆ Interpretations ◆

Dignified

In terms of personality, the Page is energetic, alert and strongly opinionated. He has a penetrating mind and possesses keen analytical skills that get swiftly to the root of any issue. This being so, he can be an excellent negotiator, particularly where subtlety and wise judgement are required. Representing a situation, this card indicates that change is on the way and that the Querant will need to make important decisions quickly and responsibly. However, it also warns of deception and points to the need for extra vigilance.

KEY THEMES
sharp intelligence • change • vigilance

Ill-dignified

The ill-dignified Page indicates someone who is cunning, devious and given to vindictive behaviour, often as a cover for his own inadequacies and shortcomings. Alternatively, the deception hinted at with the upright card is likely to be confirmed when it is reversed and the Querant should take steps to protect himself.

KEY THEMES
cunning • underhand dealings

KNIGHT OF SWORDS

KNIGHT OF SWORDS

Attributions

Element	Air
Astrological Signs	Gemini ♊
	Libra ♎
	Aquarius ♒
Life Experience	Intellectual activity

◆ INTERPRETATIONS ◆

Dignified

The upright Knight of Swords has a very forceful personality. Combining total commitment to his cause with a sharp intellect, this young man tends to be assertive to the point of being domineering: a powerful friend but a formidable opponent. When describing a situation, this card indicates that a period of strife is forthcoming but in spite of initial difficulties, the Querant is likely to triumph in the end, particularly if he adopts a decisive and positive approach from the outset.

KEY THEMES
strong personality • domineering • conflict

Ill-dignified

The reversed aspects of the Knight's personality include aggressiveness and a tendency to be impatient and headstrong. Combined, these qualities tend to exacerbate situations which call for tact and diplomacy to resolve them. This card is also said to represent a force capable of causing real harm, such as illness, natural disaster or accident.

KEY THEMES
aggression • blundering • impersonal force

QUEEN OF SWORDS

QUEEN OF SWORDS

Attributions

Element	Air
Astrological Signs	Gemini ♊
	Libra ♎
	Aquarius ♒
Life Experience	Intellectual activity

◆ INTERPRETATIONS ◆

Dignified

The Queen of Swords represents an older woman of sharp intelligence who possesses a critical mind and is highly perceptive. Often she will be a professional person in a position where she can offer counsel to others, such as the legal or teaching professions, and it is in such a capacity that she will assist the Querant. She tends to be fiercely independent and self-reliant, and perhaps as a result of this and her devotion to her work, she is often single or divorced.

KEY THEMES
a mature woman • keen perception • independent

Ill-dignified

The woman represented by this card reversed is vindictive, critical and domineering. She is something of a misanthrope (perhaps because of some blight on her personal life) and represents an important force of opposition in the Querant's life (in the professional sphere particularly), one against which he must exercise great caution.

KEY THEMES
misanthrope• hypercritical • malicious

KING OF SWORDS

KING OF SWORDS

Attributions

Element	Air
Astrological Signs	Gemini ♊
	Libra ♎
	Aquarius ♒
Life Experience	Intellectual activity

◆ INTERPRETATIONS ◆

Dignified

Authority, self-confidence and an uncompromising professionalism are all the mark of the upright King of Swords. This card tends to represent someone in business or the law who will be of great assistance to the Querant and on whom she will rely to help solve a major difficulty in her life. Assertive to the point of being domineering, this man can nevertheless be cold and remote in his interpersonal relationships and as a result, prone to feeling lonely and isolated.

KEY THEMES
a mature man • authoritative • assertive

Ill-dignified

The appearance of the ill-dignified King should act as a warning of an domineering bully in the Querant's life. This person will most likely be seeking to exploit the Querant's weaknesses and will resort to aggression where deceit and low cunning fails. Confrontation rather than appeasement will secure better results for the Querant.

KEY THEMES
bully • exploitation • confrontation

THE SUIT OF COINS

Unsurprisingly, the Suit of Coins is identified with the material aspects of our lives: wealth, possessions, finances. In a subsidiary sense, it can also be seen as representing issues relating to the Querant's status, values and sense of self-worth. Astrologically, it is associated with the feminine element of Earth.

In many ways, this particular suit may seem easier to interpret than others such as Cups or Swords, since it deals with wholly tangible concerns but there are a number of pitfalls to be wary of. Although Coins may indicate material gains or losses, it should not be automatically assumed that these will lead to the Querant's happiness or sadness. Much will depend on his or her sense of personal values and this may be reflected in the subsidiary suits which appear in the spread.

In fact, because of the matter-of-fact nature of the Coins suit, it is often only through the careful examination of subsidiary suits and how they relate to the Coins cards present that the subtler shades of meaning can be teased from the spread.

Coins represent people born under the Earth signs of Taurus, Capricorn and Virgo. If the court arcana from this suit are to be used as significators (see p.28) to represent Querants in a reading, the physical characteristics each card is traditionally associated with are given in the following table.

	HAIR	EYES
Page	Brown	Dark
Knight	Brown	Dark
Queen	Black or Dark Brown	Dark
King	Black or Dark Brown	Dark

SUIT MODIFIERS	
Opposite to Swords	Friendly with Wands/Cups

ACE OF COINS

Attributions

Element	Earth
Astrological Signs	Taurus ♉
	Capricorn ♑
	Virgo ♍
Life Aspect	Money & Material

◆ INTERPRETATIONS ◆

Dignified

All Aces signify new beginnings and the Ace of Coins indicates the beginning of an extremely productive and fulfilling period for the Querant. This is likely to involve financial gain, perhaps in the form of a windfall or possibly as a reward for a job well done. Both internal and external contentment is highlighted: in addition to the achievement of material comforts, the Querant's emotional security and the stability of the relationships around him will lead to a deep sense of satisfaction.

KEY THEMES

financial gain • recognition • emotional security

Ill-dignified

Reversed, the Ace of Coins serves as a warning against becoming too wrapped up in the acquisition of wealth. Greed, possessiveness and a poor spiritual awareness are all indicated by this card. Such traits will inevitably cause the Querant feelings of discontent, anxiety and insecurity.

KEY THEMES

materialism • self-absorption • anxiety

TWO OF COINS

Attributions

Element	Earth
Astrological Signs	Taurus ♉
	Capricorn ♑
	Virgo ♍
Life Aspect	Money & Material

◆ INTERPRETATIONS ◆

Dignified

Change is also the primary interpretation of this upright card, but not always for the better. The alteration to the Querant's material and emotional fortunes that is signified can fluctuate between positive and negative states. Problems and setbacks are likely but the Querant's strength of character and adaptability will allow her to resolve them effectively and strike a balance between competing demands upon her. Financially, this is a good card but prudent management of resources is recommended.

KEY THEMES

fluctuating fortunes • prudence

Ill-dignified

The reversed aspects of this card point to the Querant's lack of focus, indecisiveness and disorganisation when trying to cope with the changing state of her fortunes. Consequently, she may feel that she has lost control of aspects of her life and may abandon too easily plans to resolve the difficulties facing her.

KEY THEMES

loss of focus • poor self-confidence

THREE OF COINS

Attributions

Element	Earth
Astrological Signs	Taurus ♉
	Capricorn ♑
	Virgo ♍
Life Aspect	Money & Material

◆ Interpretations ◆

Dignified

The upright indications of this card mostly relate to work and the success and rightful recognition it brings the Querant. This work will be hard, will often be carried out as part of a team, and will be done on behalf of others, rather than as a personal pursuit. Clarity of purpose allied to personal skills and commitment will ultimately lead to success and a great sense of satisfaction for the Querant.

KEY THEMES

team work • success • satisfaction

Ill-dignified

Even when reversed, this card indicates hard work, except that now the outcomes will not be so favourable or rewarding for the Querant. Problems and delays will be experienced, possibly arising from his poor planning, poor delegation skills or a lack of experience. Criticism will be directed at the Querant, who (rightly or wrongly) will feel harshly treated and resentful as a consequence.

KEY THEMES

work difficulties • dissatisfaction • resentment

FOUR OF COINS

Attributions

Element	Earth
Astrological Signs	Taurus ♉
	Capricorn ♑
	Virgo ♍
Life Aspect	Money & Material

◆ INTERPRETATIONS ◆

Dignified

Upright, this card signifies a period of financial and material security for the Querant. This may be underpinned by the receipt of a substantial gift or an inheritance. It may also be the consequence of successful commercial dealings, where the Querant's hard work and business acumen result in an increase in her status, power and material rewards. The Querant is likely to feel that both her material and her emotional needs are being met.

KEY THEMES
security • contentment

Ill-dignified

In its reversed orientation, this card points to the problems of an overattachment to material wealth and possessions: greed, avarice, and miserliness. The fear of loss (of power as well as wealth) is a major concern for the Querant and is preventing her making much-needed changes in her life (surrounding cards will indicate particular areas this affects).

KEY THEMES
miserliness • fear of loss • indecisiveness

FIVE OF COINS

Attributions

Element	Earth
Astrological Signs	Taurus ♉
	Capricorn ♑
	Virgo ♍
Life Aspect	Money & Material

◆ INTERPRETATIONS ◆

Dignified

This is not a good card to draw as all its indicators point to hardship. Financial difficulty is certainly indicated, possibly resulting from unemployment. Problems with relationships may also be prevalent, with illicit affairs, unsatisfying emotional ties or simply a general lack of love in the Querant's life being at their root. Inevitably, such conditions lead to feelings of insecurity and anxiety, but by prioritising his affairs, the Querant may be able take positive steps to limit the extent of these problems.

KEY THEMES

emotional and financial difficulties • worry

Ill-dignified

Problems generally associated with this card will be more severe or more prolonged when it is reversed. The Querant's health may also be suffering as a result. Given this, the need to understand or acknowledge the full extent of the problems will be an important first step in tackling them.

KEY THEMES

severe hardships • health problems

Six of Coins

Attributions

Element	Earth
Astrological Signs	Taurus ♉
	Capricorn ♑
	Virgo ♍
Life Aspect	Money & Material

✦ INTERPRETATIONS ✦

Dignified

The upright Six points to success and prosperity going hand-in-hand with generosity and benevolence. The card indicates that the Querant will achieve much success and reward in the commercial field which will bring her satisfaction and security. It also points to a generous and philanthropic trait in the Querant's nature which will lead to acts of charity or patronage. Alternatively, it may indicate that she will be on the receiving end of this generosity.

KEY THEMES
prosperity • solvency • charitable acts

Ill-dignified

Reversed, the positive aspects of generosity are transformed into financial recklessness and the squandering of resources. Loss is indicated generally, not simply of material things but perhaps of emotional ties. This may be the result of theft or care-lessness on the part of the Querant but it may also stem from the jealous, underhand actions of others.

KEY THEMES
financial recklessness • loss • enmity

SEVEN OF COINS

Attributions

Element	Earth
Astrological Signs	Taurus ♉
	Capricorn ♑
	Virgo ♍
Life Aspect	Money & Material

◆ Interpretations ◆

Dignified

Upright, this card signifies limited success. Hard work and sustained effort will eventually bring sought-after returns for the Querant but these may seem a long way off at the moment. He will be facing setbacks to projects and speculations which in many ways are the result of his overcautiousness. Anxiety and a fear of failing result from, but also exacerbate, this cautious approach. Yet if the Querant perseveres, his hard work will be rewarded in the longer term.

KEY THEMES

perseverance • long-term success

Ill-dignified

The reversed aspects of this card suggest lost opportunities, frustration, and despondency. The Querant will lose heart at the slow progress of current projects or succumb to the problems facing him. Enterprises will be abandoned which will undoubtedly result in financial loss. This card cautions the Querant against making such hasty business decisions.

KEY THEMES

abandoned opportunities • rash decisions

EIGHT OF COINS

Attributions

Element	Earth
Astrological Signs	Taurus ♉
	Capricorn ♑
	Virgo ♍
Life Aspect	Money & Material

◆ INTERPRETATIONS ◆

Dignified

Upright, the Eight signifies the successful application of creative or craft skills by the Querant. These may be newly learned and may not be her main employment but the satisfaction she derives from them go beyond any financial benefits they bring. The card also indicates financial prudence and a degree of caution as the Querant goes about her affairs, and suggests that organisation, attention to detail and preparation will secure the desired results.

KEY THEMES
craftsmanship • new skills • prudence

Ill-dignified

Reversed, this card indicates a lack of ambition and wasted opportunites for personal growth. The Querant is too absorbed with everyday concerns and worries to be able to assess properly what needs to be done to achieve long-term security. Energy and opportunities will be wasted pursuing short-term gains and quick, but small, returns on effort.

KEY THEMES
wasted opportunites • self-absorption

NINE OF COINS

Attributions

Element	Earth
Astrological Signs	Taurus ♉
	Capricorn ♑
	Virgo ♍
Life Aspect	Money & Material

✦ INTERPRETATIONS ✦

Dignified

The upright Nine signifies considerable material success, financial security and achievement. These may have been attained as a result of much effort and follow periods of hardship, which makes them all the more appreciated. However, solitude is also indicated by this card so it may be that the Querant is enjoying the fruits of his labours alone. This may be welcomed by him but it is possible that it signifies that he is still seeking an elusive emotional security.

KEY THEMES

material security • solitude

Ill-dignified

When reversed, this card carries a warning that current material security and comfort may be under threat. This may be because the foundations on which this security was established are transitory and about to change, or because of repercussions arising from the Querant's past conduct (possibly illegal or at least morally dubious).

KEY THEMES

material security compromised • dubious practices

TEN OF COINS

Attributions

Element	Earth
Astrological Signs	Taurus ♉
	Capricorn ♑
	Virgo ♍
Life Aspect	Money & Material

◆ INTERPRETATIONS ◆

Dignified

Both material prosperity and emotional security feature strongly amongst the Ten's upright indicators. Here, however, this security is closely bound up with family relationships or close friendships. It may be that the foundations of the Querant's current prosperity were laid by previous members of her family or that she has received, or is about to, an inheritance. The Querant will feel strongly bound by these ties and there will be a mutually beneficial flow of advice and financial assistance between them.

KEY THEMES
prosperity • close relationships • inheritance

Ill-dignified

The family ties which were the strength of the upright Ten now become a weakness when reversed. Family or close friends may be imposing restrictions or responsibilities on the Querant (knowingly or not), or may be the source of financial disputes and problems for her.

KEY THEMES
family disputes • financial difficulties

PAGE OF COINS

Attributions

Element Earth
Astrological Signs Taurus ♉
Capricorn ♑
Virgo ♍
Life Aspect Money & Material

◆ Interpretations ◆

Dignified

Characteristics associated with this card are those of scholarship, application of effort, conscientiousness and introspection. The creative or psychic arts are also indicated so these characteristics may apply particularly in these fields. The Page of Coins generally signifies good news for the Querant or a young person close to him. This may take the form of exam results or promotions, or concern financial matters. A very positive meeting with someone who shares the Querant's outlook is also highlighted.

KEY THEMES
scholarship • good news • creativity

Ill-dignified

The reversed characteristics of the Page of Coins focus on a lack of application where it is needed, and a pedantry and pettiness where it is not. The Querant or a young person close to him is wasteful of the opportunites presented to them. Bad news, particularly about money issues, is also indicated.

KEY THEMES
idleness • pettiness • money problems

KNIGHT OF COINS

KNIGHT OF COINS

Attributions

Element	Earth
Astrological Signs	Taurus ♉
	Capricorn ♑
	Virgo ♍
Life Aspect	Money & Material

✦ INTERPRETATIONS ✦

Dignified

Character indicators for the upright Knight include dependability, persistence, patience and trustworthiness, traditionally signifying a young man with a responsible, if cautious, approach to life. He may be the Querant's employee or engaged by him for a particular job; the upright Knight suggests that the task will be done to the Querant's satisfaction. It may also point to the arrival of positive news for the Querant regarding money, travel or business, brought by a young man.

KEY THEMES
thoroughness • dependability • good news

Ill-dignified

Reversed, the Knight's cautious characteristics may develop into inertia, timidity and ineffectiveness, and signify an unmotivated young man. The card can indicate that progress in the Querant's financial and business affairs has slowed and is in danger of stagnating unless a new approach is sought.

KEY THEMES
timid nature • stagnation • new approaches

QUEEN OF COINS

QUEEN OF COINS

Attributions

Element	Earth
Astrological Signs	Taurus ♉
	Capricorn ♑
	Virgo ♍
Life Aspect	Money & Material

◆ INTERPRETATIONS ◆

Dignified

The Queen of Coins signifies a practical, down-to-earth woman who tends to be home- and family-oriented. She can also possess a shrewdness of judgement (particularly in financial matters) and a capacity for hard work which makes her equally successful in business. This card points to a mature woman who will assist the Querant with her money affairs, either with good advice or financial help.

KEY THEMES

practicality • shrewdness • financial help

Ill-dignified

Reversed, the Queen signifies an overly materialistic and suspicious nature and a tendency towards conspicuous consumption. It can indicate a mature woman causing problems for the Querant, particularly over money. She is likely to be someone who is deeply insecure, the outward manifestations of which include greed, and displays of wealth and social standing.

KEY THEMES

materialism • insecurity • conflict

KING OF COINS

KING OF COINS

Attributions

Element	Earth
Astrological Signs	Taurus ♉
	Capricorn ♑
	Virgo ♍
Life Aspect	Money & Material

◆ INTERPRETATIONS ◆

Dignified

The King of Coins traditionally signifies a reliable, practical, mature man, someone who, by his own efforts, has achieved success and status in his field (which is likely to be numerate – possibly banking or stockbroking). Although successful, this person is likely to be somewhat cautious in approach and perhaps not particularly intelligent. The upright King can signify an improvement in the Querant's financial security and possibly promotion at work.

KEY THEMES
reliability • success • security

Ill-dignified

The reversed King is another card signifying a pre-occupation with material wealth. It usually indicates a mature male who is stupid, lacking in sensitivity and rather shallow. In spite of this, he may be a strong and forceful character and may be someone who is opposing the Querant, perhaps over a financial or work-related issue, and motivated by jealousy.

KEY THEMES
insensitive • overly materialistic

FURTHER READING

The following reading list is intended to provide a starting point for those who wish to extend their knowledge of tarot beyond the brief introduction offered by this book.

Although many of the following books are considered 'classics' on their subject, you may find that some are no longer in print or difficult to obtain in high street bookshops. Major libraries are likely to stock many of them or should at least be able to obtain them for you. Alternatively, you could try any of the bookshops listed on p.252.

Abraham, Sylvia *How to Read the Tarot: The Keyword System* Llewellyn Publications, USA 1974

Benares, Camden *Common Sense Tarot* Newcastle Publishing Co., USA 1992

Case, Paul Foster *The Tarot: A Key to the Wisdom of the Ages* The Banton Press, USA 1993

Connolly, Eileen *Tarot – the Complete Handbook for the Apprentice* Thorsons, London 1979; 1995 edition

Connolly, Eileen *Tarot – the Handbook for the Journeyman* Thorsons, London 1990

Crowley, Aleister *Tarot Divination* Samuel Weiser Inc., New York 1977

Gordon, Richard *Intuitive Tarot: A Metaphysical Approach to Reading the Tarot* Blue Dolphin Publishing, USA 1994

Kaplan, Stuart *Classical Tarot: Its Origins, Meanings and Divinatory Uses* Thoth Publications/Aquarian Press, Wellingborough 1989

Kaplan, Stuart *The Encyclopedia of the Tarot* US Games Systems, New York 1993

Kelly, Dorothy *Tarot Card Combinations* Samuel Weiser Inc., New York 1995

Lellieux, David *Ancient Tarot and its Symbolism* Cornwall Books, USA 1985

Muchery, Georges *Astrological Tarot* Senate Publishing, USA 1994

Ouspensky P.D. *The Symbolism of the Tarot* Dover Publications, New York 1976

Peach, Emily *Discover Tarot: Understanding and Using Tarot Symbolism* Aquarian Press, Wellingborough 1990

Pollack, Rachael *Seventy-eight Degrees of Wisdom* (2 vols) Thoth Publications/Aquarian Press, Wellingborough 1980

Pollack, Rachael *Tarot Readings and Meditation* Aquarian Press/Thorsons, Wellingborough 1990

Pollack, Rachel *The New Tarot – Modern Variations of Ancient Images* Aquarian Press/Thorsons, Wellingborough 1989

Prosapio, Richard *Intuitive Tarot* Morgan & Morgan, USA 1990

Sandor, Konradd *Classical Tarot Spreads* Whitford Press, USA 1985

Waite, Arthur E. *A Pictorial Key to the Tarot* Citadel Press, USA 1980

Walker, Ann *Living Tarot* Capall Bann Publishing, USA 1994

Walker, Barbara G. *The Secrets of the Tarot: Origins, History & Symbolism* Harper & Row, New York 1984

USEFUL ADDRESSES

As with the reading list on the preceding pages, the following is not intended to be exhaustive. However, most readers' requirements should be catered for using the contacts offered here.

CARD SUPPLIERS

R. Somerville of Edinburgh
82 Canongate
The Royal Mile
Edinburgh
EH8 8BZ

Ph: 0131-556 5225
Fx: 0131-557 9305
E-mail: cards@playing-cards.demon.co.uk
web site: www.playing-cards.demon.co.uk

U.S. Games Systems Inc.
179 Ludlow St
Stamford
CT 06902
USA

Ph: 00 1 203 353 8400
Fx: 00 1 203 353 8431
E-mail: usgames@aol.com

For a small fee ($2.00), U.S. Games will send you a full-colour, 64 page catalogue of their very extensive range of tarot decks.

BOOKSHOPS AND SUPPLIERS OF TAROT ACCESSORIES

Pentagram
11 Cheapside
Wakefield
WF1 2SD

Ph: 01294-298930
Fx: 01294-298930
E-mail: pentagram@psinet.demon.co.uk
web site: www.psinet.co.uk

Mysteries
9–11 Monmouth St
Covent Garden
London
WC2H 9DA

Ph: 0171-240 3688

Watkins Bookshop
21 Cecil Court
Leicester Sq.
London
WC2N 4EZ

Ph: 0171-836 2182
Fax: 0171-836 6700

CORRESPONDENCE COURSES

The London Tarot Centre
25 Gisburn Rd
Hornsey
London
N8 7BS

Ph: 0181-340 3788
Fax: 0181-348 8665

TAROT ON THE INTERNET

If you have access to the Internet and the Web, then you will find literally thousands of sites devoted to various aspects of tarot. Many of these offer readings and should generally be avoided but many others are informative and fun. The Internet is also extremely handy when it comes to

ordering cards, books and other accessories
(which is why I've included website addresses
where they are available for the suppliers listed
above).

COLLINS GEM

COLLINS GEM

Bestselling Collins Gem titles include:

Gem English Dictionary (£3.99)

Gem Thesaurus (£3.99)

Gem French Dictionary (£3.99)

Gem German Dictionary (£3.99)

Gem Calorie Counter (£3.50)

Gem Basic Facts Mathematics (£3.99)

Gem SAS Survival Guide (£3.99)

Gem Babies' Names (£3.50)

Gem Card Games (£3.99)

Gem Ready Reference (£3.99)

All Collins Gems are available from your local bookseller or can b ordered directly from the publishers.

In the UK, contact Mail Order, Dept 2A, HarperCollins Publisher Westerhill Rd, Bishopbriggs, Glasgow, G64 2QT, listing the title required and enclosing a cheque or p.o. for the value of the books pl £1.00 for the first title and 25p for each additional title to cover p& Access and Visa cardholders can order on 0141-772 2281 (24 hr).

In Australia, contact Customer Services, HarperCollins Distributi Yarrawa Rd, Moss Vale 2577 (tel. [048] 68 0300). **In New Zealar** contact Customer Services, HarperCollins Publishers, 31 View F Glenfield, Auckland 10 (tel. [09] 444 3740). **In Canada**, contact your lo bookshop.

All prices quoted are correct at time of going to press.